Creative
Pattern
Skills
for fashion design

Creative
Pattern
Skills
for fashion design

Bernard Zamkoff
Professor & Former Chairman
Fashion Design Department—Apparel
Fashion Institute of Technology

Jeanne Price
Professor
Fashion Design Department—Apparel
Fashion Institute of Technology

Fairchild Publications
New York

Bina Abling, artist: Title Sketches
Kathleen Ashenfelter, artist: Diagrams
Delgado Design Inc.: Book Design

F.I.T.
COLLECTION

Standard Book Number: 87005-682-4

Library of Congress Catalog Card Number: 89-82494

Printed in the United States of America

Preface

Flat pattern design can be as creative a method of producing fashion as any other discipline, while offering speed and accuracy, as well as inspiration, to the designer. In our companion text, *Basic Pattern Skills for Fashion Design*, the major sections of a garment were studied, and the essential methods of flat pattern design were explained. Now in this text, *Creative Pattern Skills for Fashion Design*, we are combining those major sections into new structures, such as the sleeve and bodice in one piece, or with only a partial armhole, and the collar and bodice combinations of the shawl and notch collars. All of these combined sections are explained and demonstrated on both the waist-length bodice and the hip-length garment, as well as being shown on both fitted and loose silhouettes.

Each section begins with a discussion of the theory behind the particular sleeve or collar being introduced. This is followed by step-by-step instructions for creating the basic draft of that design, and several variations on that basic design as well. Once those steps are understood, you can then go on to the next area, which is a collection of designs and patterns that further explore the variations possible within that sleeve or collar. These designs can serve as inspiration for your own creative ideas, as well as excellent practice lessons for each theory presented. Therefore, using this book you can first learn the "why" behind each sleeve and collar, then do the actual steps necessary to make the basic shapes, and finally, interpret actual designs based on those basic shapes. This sequence is followed for each shape introduced, and it is a system that we believe is unique to this book in the field of flat pattern design. For that matter, we are equally certain that our methods are as unique as our format, and that they offer the clearest and quickest techniques yet devised.

The main sections of this book are: the kimono family of sleeves, which includes the dolman, batwing, and gusset; the semi-set-in family of sleeves, which includes the raglan, yoke, princess, and dropped shoulder; and the shawl and notch collars. Each section includes the theory, drafts, designs and patterns described above, and together they can take you past basic knowledge into the exciting and challenging world of advanced, and creative flat pattern design.

1990

Bernard Zamkoff
Jeanne Price

New York

Contents

Creative
Pattern
Skills
for fashion design

Sleeves-in-One with the Bodice

The five basic sleeve silhouettes are illustrated here. This portion of the text focuses on the **Dolman, Kimono, Gusset,** and **Semi-Set-in Sleeves;** the Set-in Sleeve is discussed thoroughly in our companion text, *Basic Pattern Skills for Fashion Design.*

One approach to understanding these sleeves is to divide them into two categories: informal or sporty sleeves which allow for freedom of arm movement, and formal or tailored sleeves which somewhat restrict arm movement in favor of a more fitted look.

The Kimono is the informal, looser sleeve from which the Dolman and the Gusset Sleeves are created. The "Big Shirt" is an even looser version of these sleeves, in which the darts are used as ease.

The Set-in Sleeve is the formal and more fitted sleeve from which the Semi-Set-in sleeve is created.

The Kimono, Dolman and Gusset sleeves can be cut in one-piece with the bodice, while the Set-in and Semi-Set-in sleeves always have a seam separating the sleeve from the bodice.

The first basic sleeve silhouette discussed is the Kimono.

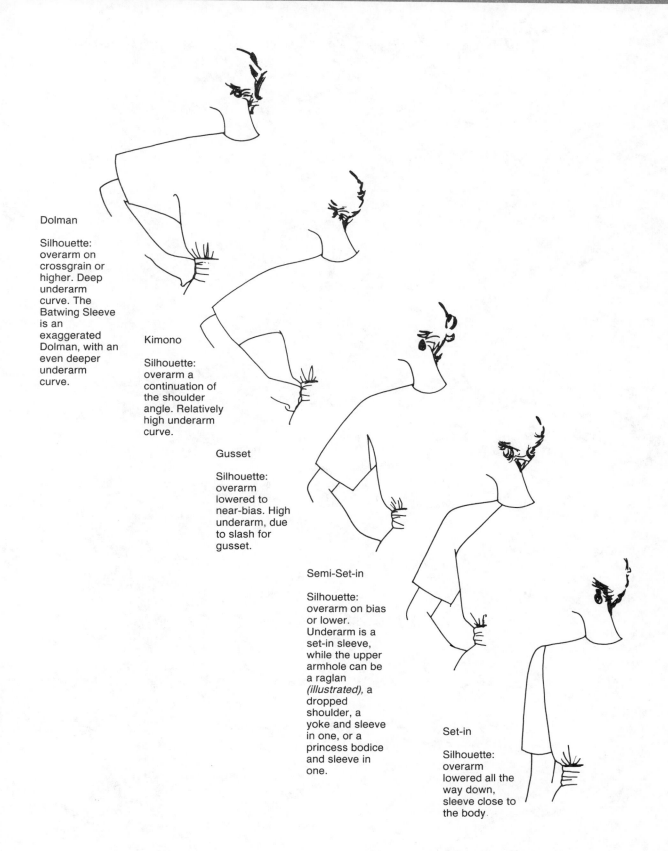

Dolman

Silhouette: overarm on crossgrain or higher. Deep underarm curve. The Batwing Sleeve is an exaggerated Dolman, with an even deeper underarm curve.

Kimono

Silhouette: overarm a continuation of the shoulder angle. Relatively high underarm curve.

Gusset

Silhouette: overarm lowered to near-bias. High underarm, due to slash for gusset.

Semi-Set-in

Silhouette: overarm on bias or lower. Underarm is a set-in sleeve, while the upper armhole can be a raglan *(illustrated),* a dropped shoulder, a yoke and sleeve in one, or a princess bodice and sleeve in one.

Set-in

Silhouette: overarm lowered all the way down, sleeve close to the body.

One

The Kimono Sleeve

Kimono Sleeve/Theory

1

Front half of a
set-in sleeve

2

3

Lost overarm
length

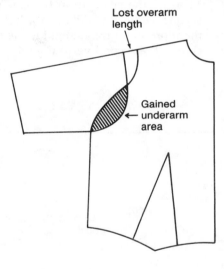

Gained
underarm
area

4

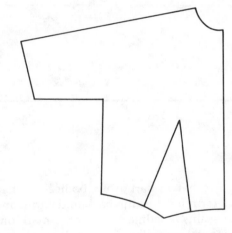

In theory, the kimono sleeve can be created by pivoting a set-in sleeve into an outward silhouette **(illustrations 1–4).** This outward silhouette allows for freer arm movement than does the fitted set-in sleeve, because the underarm has more area, or lift, than the set-in sleeve has, while the overarm has less length. The kimono and set-in sleeves are therefore opposite silhouettes; one outward, informal and loose, and the other downward, formal and fitted.

The following pages describe the actual steps needed to create a perfectly balanced front and back elbow-length kimono sleeve.

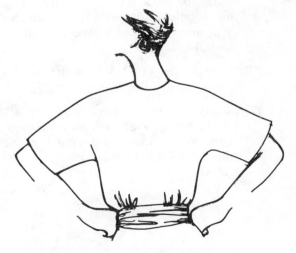

Kimono Silhouette

Kimono Sleeve & Fitted Bodice

1

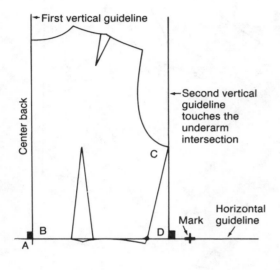

To create balanced kimono sleeves, both the underarms and the shoulders must be balanced front to back.

A Draw a horizontal guideline, and square a vertical guideline from it.

B Place the back bodice so that its center back/waistline intersection fits into the intersection of the guidelines.

C Square up a second vertical guideline that touches the back underarm intersection.

D Measure the space from the side seam to the second vertical guideline. Mark that measurement on the horizontal guideline on the other side of the second vertical guideline.

2

A Place the two-dart front bodice so that its underarm touches the back underarm, and its side seam/waistline touches the mark on the horizontal guideline. (The center front/waistline should also touch that guideline.) The underarms are now balanced on the second vertical guideline.

B Trace the front bodice from the shoulder dart to one-third of the armhole.

C Square a line from the second vertical guideline to the back shoulder, and measure that space. Repeat that measurement on the other side of the second vertical guideline, and place a mark.

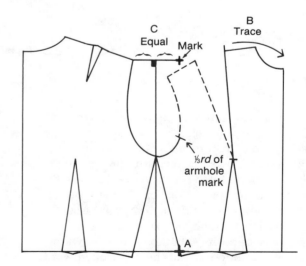

3

A Pivot the front shoulder dart toward center front until the end of the shoulder touches, or lines up with, the mark. (See Step 4 if it just lines up with the mark.) Trace from one-third of the armhole to the shoulder dart.

B Fold and true (with a tracing wheel) the new, smaller front shoulder dart.

C The front and back shoulders are now balanced on the second vertical guideline.

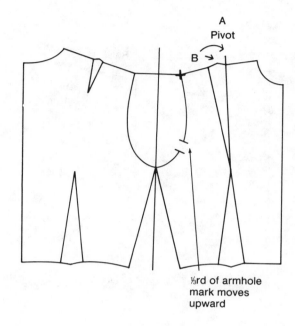

⅓rd of armhole
mark moves
upward

4

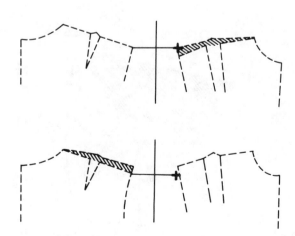

A If the pivoted shoulder corner lines up *below* the mark, extend the armhole up to the mark and true in a new front shoulder seam.

B If the pivoted shoulder corner lines up *above* the mark, raise the back shoulder an equal amount, and true in a new back shoulder seam.

Kimono Sleeve & Fitted Bodice

5

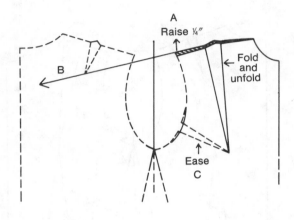

A Whether or not any adjustments were necessary as in Step 4, now raise the front shoulder ¼" for ease. Draw a new shoulder to the neck, folding the shoulder dart closed while doing so. Unfold the dart after the new shoulder is drawn.

B Extend the new front shoulder line as a straight line of indefinite length. This line will serve as a guideline for the shoulder seam of the kimono sleeve.

C The amount of space pivoted into the first third of the front armhole is left in as ease. Blend a new armhole across the open space.

6

A Using the front half of an elbow-length set-in sleeve, touch its bicep corner to the bodice underarm. Pivot the sleeve up until its center line is parallel to the indefinite line.

B Trace the sleeve's underarm and elbow edges.

C Extend the elbow edge up to the indefinite line, which creates a square corner. The front kimono bodice is now complete (heavy lines).

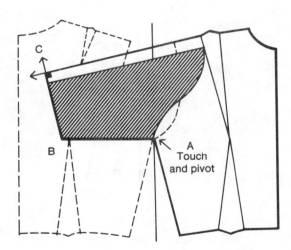

7

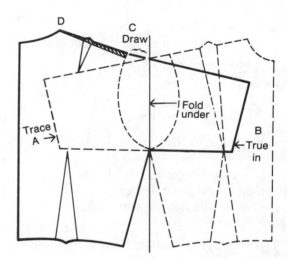

A Fold the front bodice under on the second vertical guideline, and trace the part of the front sleeve that was drawn over the back bodice.

B Unfold, and true in the tracing to create the back kimono sleeve (heavy lines).

C Draw in the shoulder section, from the vertical guideline to the back shoulder, that was not traced.

D This last drawn line will end ¼" above the back shoulder. Connect it to the back neck, folding the shoulder dart closed while doing so, to create a new back shoulder with the same ¼" ease as the front shoulder.

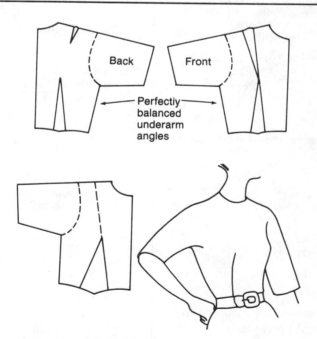

Kimono Front with Waist Dart

The back underarm angle will still perfectly match the front underarm angle, but the grains of the underarm and overarm seams will no longer match.

Kimono Sleeve with Armhole Seam

1

Kimono sleeve & bodice separated

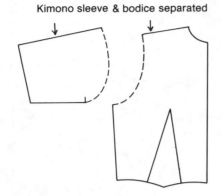

Whenever an armhole seam is used in a kimono design, a "hook" can be created at the underarm which gives greater lift, by making the underarm seam longer.

A Trace the bodice section of the kimono sleeve.

B Trace the sleeve section separately.

C Repeat A and B for the back section.

D The bodice section can be styled as desired.

2

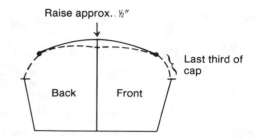

Raise approx. ½"

Last third of cap

Back   Front

A Place the front and back sections of the sleeve together. (Sleeve can be any length.)

B Raise the cap approximately ½" to create a smoothly curved cap. This raised cap also removes some of the pull to the shoulder caused by the shortened cap of the kimono sleeve.

C Connect the ½" to the last third of the cap, front and back, in a smooth curve.

3

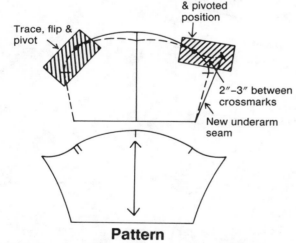

Trace, flip & pivot

Paper in flipped & pivoted position

2"–3" between crossmarks

New underarm seam

Pattern

A Trace the last third of the front cap on a separate piece of paper.

B Flip the paper over, touch the "last third" marks to each other, and pivot the tracing up between 2 to 3 inches. Trace the raised armhole. Draw a gently curved new underarm seam to the elbow line.

C Repeat all steps for the back. Be certain that the new underarm seams are balanced.

Quick Method

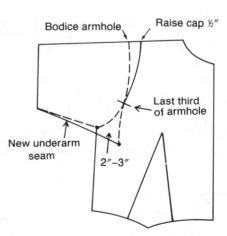

Bodice armhole   Raise cap ½"

Last third of armhole

New underarm seam

2"–3"

Steps 1, 2 and 3 can be applied directly to a kimono sleeve without separating the bodice and sleeve (illustrated). After completing the separate front and back sleeves, they can be joined into one piece when they are traced off as a pattern.

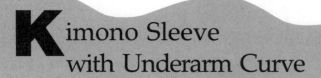

Kimono Sleeve with Underarm Curve

. . . Or By Crook

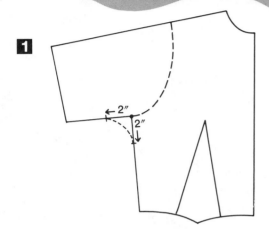

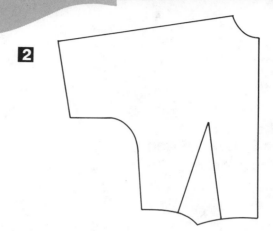

The pointed underarm intersection is not always desirable on a one-piece kimono; the slash into the seam allowance, which is necessary for sewing weakens the corner. A curve, however, has several slashes, which distributes the weak points around the curve and thus lessens the impact. Also, a curve will be on the bias, which eases the strain on the curve when the arm is raised. For a curved underarm, measure out 2" equally onto the undearm and side seams, from the underarm intersection. Connect with a smooth curve.

Since the curve actually reduces the length of the underarm seam, it also tends to reduce the lift. Therefore, a curve deeper than 2" by 2" should be avoided. (For curves deeper than that, see the **Dolman Sleeve, page 44.**) Repeat all steps for the back sleeve.

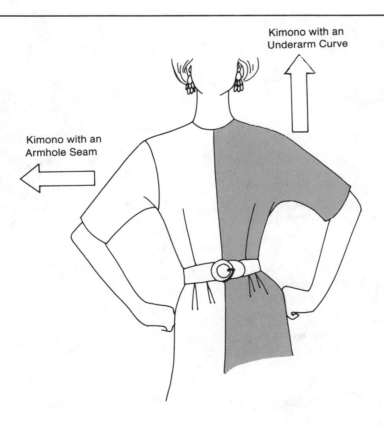

Kimono with an Underarm Curve

Kimono with an Armhole Seam

Long Kimono Sleeve
—Fitted or Straight

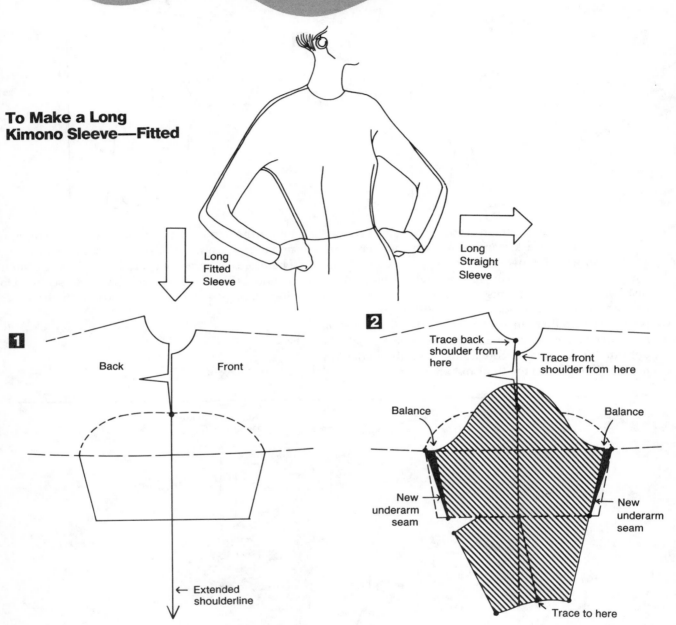

**To Make a Long
Kimono Sleeve—Fitted**

Long
Fitted
Sleeve

Long
Straight
Sleeve

1

Back   Front

← Extended
shoulderline

2

Trace back
shoulder from
here

Trace front
shoulder from here

Balance

Balance

New
underarm
seam

New
underarm
seam

Trace to here

A Trace the waist-darted front and back kimono sleeve-bodice in a shoulder to shoulder position. (The back and front may overlap from armhole to neck, or there may be a gap; either of which is not important since the sleeves will be cut separately.)

B Extend the shoulderline indefinitely downward past the elbow.

A Place the center of a set-in sleeve on the extended shoulderline balancing it on the kimono's bicep line. Trace the sleeve.

B Connect bodices' underarms to sleeves' elbow line, to create new underarm seams.

C Trace the bodices and sleeve as separate front and back sections, tracing the bodices along their shoulders down to the center of the fitted wrist (see dots).

D After the bodices are separated, the back shoulder dart may be pivoted into the neck.

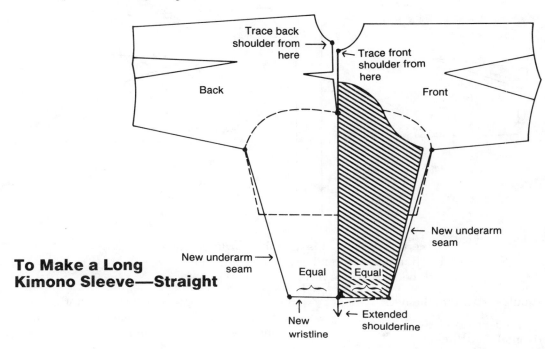

Long Straight Sleeve

Trace back
shoulder from →
here

← Trace front
shoulder from
here

Back

Front

New underarm
seam

**To Make a Long
Kimono Sleeve—Straight**

New underarm →
seam

Equal

Equal

New
wristline

← Extended
shoulderline

A Complete Steps 1 and 2A, **page 14,** tracing only the front of the set-in sleeve.

B Square a line from the extended shoulderline to the front wrist corner. Measure this squared line, and repeat the measurement on the other side of the extended shoulderline, on a continuation of the squared line.

C Connect this new wristline to the front and back bodice underarm intersections, and trace the bodices and sleeve as separate front and back sections (see dots).

D Once the bodices are separated, the back shoulder dart may be pivoted into the neck, and the front waist dart can be distributed into a shoulder and waist dart, if desired.

Note: This sleeve has the narrowest wrist possible without needing an elbow dart to shape the sleeve, which a narrower wrist would require.

Kimono Sleeve- Bodice in One Piece

1

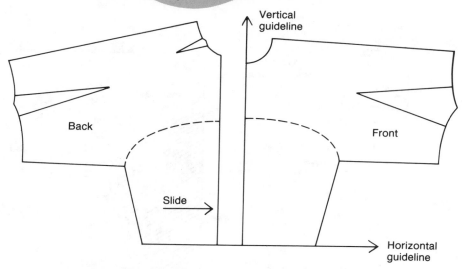

For certain designs, it is desirable to eliminate the shoulder seam and to cut the front and back bodices as one piece.

A Pivot the back shoulder dart into the neck.

B Place the front shoulder and elbow lines on vertical and horizontal guidelines.

C Slide the back elbow line along the horizontal guideline until the back overarm seam lies against the front underarm seam.

2

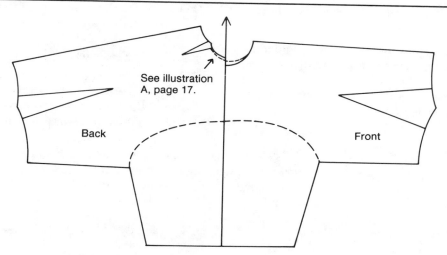

A The back neck may or may not touch the vertical guideline. If it does, it may not touch the front neckline at the same position. In that case, design a new compromised neckline through the center of the difference at the vertical guideline. See A, **page 17.**)

B If the back neck does not touch the guideline, follow instructions for **B, page 17.**

C If the back neckline overlaps the front neckline, follow instructions for **C, page 17.**

D Trace the front and back kimono bodices as a one-piece pattern.

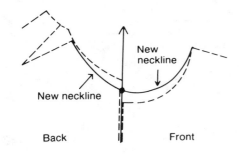

Back   Front

A If the back and front shoulders touch, but the necklines do not touch, draw a compromised neckline. The black dot represents the center of the difference between the front and back neckline, through which the compromised new neckline is drawn.

Space added to
the back
neckline is
divided & used
to make the
neck dart wider

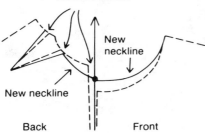

Back   Front

B If the front and back shoulders and the necklines do not touch, draw a compromised neckline through the center of the difference (black dot). Divide the space added to the back neckline on both sides of the back neck dart, making it wider to compensate for the longer neckline. Draw a new, wider neck dart.

Space lost in
the back
neckline is
divided & used
to make the
neck dart
narrower

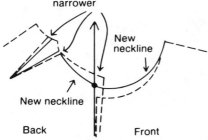

Back   Front

C If the back shoulder overlaps the front shoulder at the neckline, draw a compromised neckline (black dot). Divide the space lost in the back neckline on both sides of the inside of the back neck dart, making it narrower to compensate for the shorter neckline. Draw a new, narrower neck dart.

Kimono-Raglan Sleeve

The kimono-raglan, developed from the one-piece kimono (**pages 16** and **17**), retains the kimono's loose silhouette, and combines it with the raglan's look of a seam from the underarm to the neck. In addition, whenever a kimono-raglan sleeve seam is designed to touch the armhole of the pattern, it becomes possible to lengthen and raise the underarm seam for greater ease and lift.

1

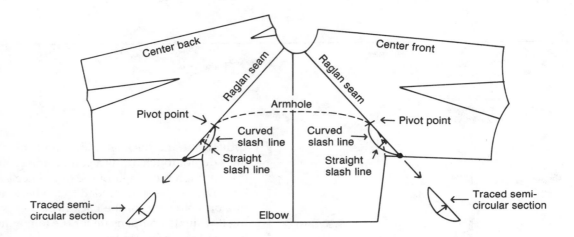

A Design raglan seams from the front and back neck towards the side seams (black dots) that just touch the armhole.

B Crossmark the points where the raglan seams touch the armhole. Mark those points as the pivot points.

C Draw semi-circular slash lines from the pivot points to the end of each raglan seam (black dots), making the curves approximately 1½″ deep at their widest point. Draw a straight slash line from the widest point of each curve to the raglan seam.

D Trace the semi-circular sections, and cut them out; cut the straight slash lines.

2

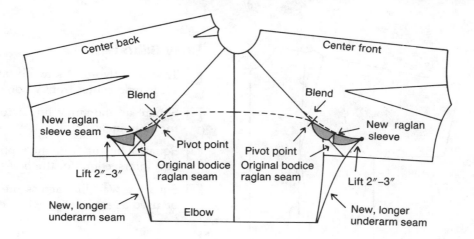

A Match the traced semi-circular sections to the pivot points and lift the corners up 2″ to 3″ or as desired, on front and back. Blend the pivot points. The straight slash lines will spread open to help create smoothly curved new raglan sleeve seams.

B Draw new, curved underarm seams from the lifted raglan seams (black dots) to the elbow line, or to the hem edge when the sleeve is shorter than elbow length.

C The bodices are traced around the original raglan seams. The sleeves are traced around the raised raglan seams. When sewn, the difference in length between the new curved and the original straight underarm seams results in a sleeve with a higher lift.
Principle: The longer the underarm seam, the higher the lift.

Patterns

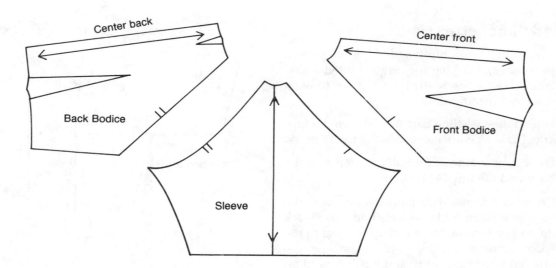

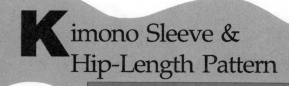

Kimono Sleeve & Hip-Length Pattern

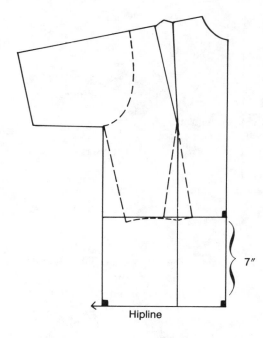

7"

Hipline

Boxy Silhouette

A Trace the two-dart kimono bodice, **pages 10–11**. Extend center front 7" downward.

B Square an indefinite line across the 7" point, for a hipline.

C Square a line up from the hipline to the under-arm intersection, for the boxy side seam.

D Square a waistline across the center front, to be used as a guideline when designing.

Fitted Silhouette

A Create the boxy hip-length kimono pattern (see above), marking the original fitted waist-length bodice inside the boxy pattern (broken lines in illustration).

B Extend the waistline dart to 1" above the hip-line. Draw a gently curved dart to the 1" mark.

C Draw a new side seam halfway between the boxy and the fitted side seam.

D Create a second dart halfway between the new side seam and the waistline dart (black dots). The second dart's pickup is equal to the space between the new side seam and the original fitted side seam, and it is balanced on a vertical guideline drawn squared to the waistline at the halfway point. Begin the new dart 1" below the apex level of the waistline dart, and end it 3⅛" above the hipline.

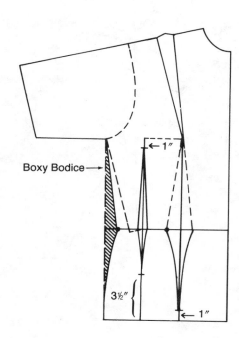

Boxy Bodice→

←1"

3½"

←1"

Semi-Fitted Silhouette

A Create the boxy hip-length kimono pattern, as shown on **page 20** marking the original fitted waist-length bodice inside the boxy pattern (broken lines in illustration).

B Reduce the waistline dart pickup by half.

C Extend the dart to 2″ above the hipline. Draw in the narrowed dart.

D Draw a new side seam in from the boxy side seam, approximately one-fourth of the distance toward the fitted side seam.

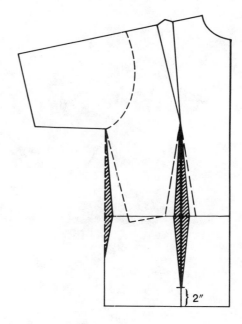

Flared Silhouette

Using the boxy pattern, pivot the shoulder dart into the hem, and blend. In all these diagrams, the solid lines indicate the finished pattern and their darts. The back patterns are created in the same manner as the front (for an example of back flare see **page 40**).

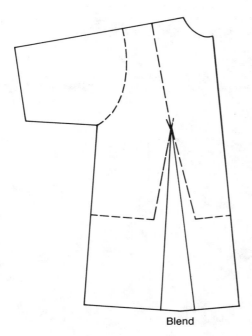

Blend

Design Variations

Kimono-Raglan Sleeve

Design Features

- Fitted front-wrapped kimono-raglan with tucks at waistline
- Elbow-length kimono sleeves

Basic Patterns

- The Kimono Sleeve & Fitted Bodice, **pages 8–11**
- The Kimono Sleeve with Underarm Curve, **page 13**

Drafts

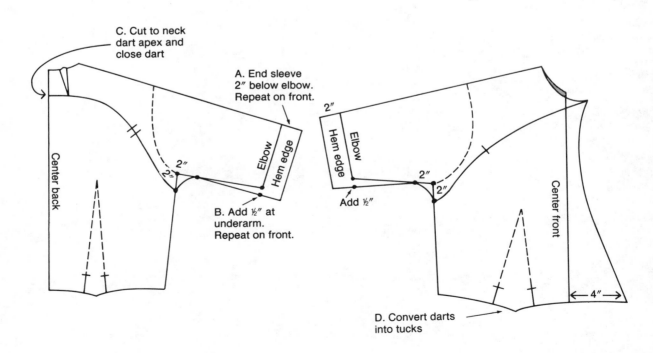

C. Cut to neck dart apex and close dart

A. End sleeve 2″ below elbow. Repeat on front.

Center back

Elbow

Hem edge

2″

2″

B. Add ½″ at underarm. Repeat on front.

2″

Hem edge

Elbow

Add ½″

2″

2″

Center front

D. Convert darts into tucks

4″

Patterns

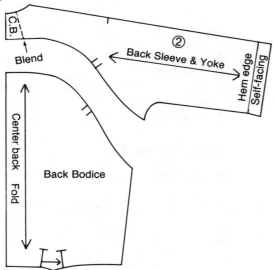

C.B.

Blend

② Back Sleeve & Yoke

Hem edge
Self-facing

Center back   Fold

Back Bodice

Facings and hems have not always been indicated in this text, but they are to be considered as choices for finishing the various raw edges. Al! measurements given are suggestions only, and may be varied as desired.

D E S I G N   V A R I A T I O N

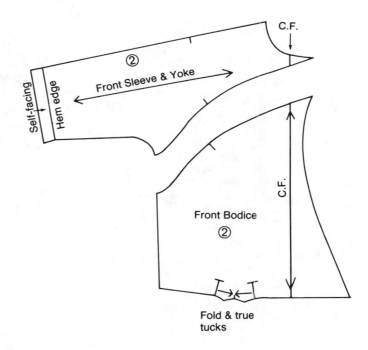

C.F.

②

Self-facing

Hem edge

Front Sleeve & Yoke

C.F.

Front Bodice
②

Fold & true
tucks

Kimono-Raglan Sleeve

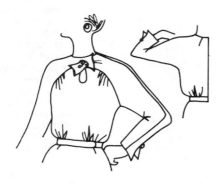

Design Features

- ▪ Kimono sleeve with raglan-style seam in front only
- ▪ Shaped placket at sleeve wrist with loop and button closing
- ▪ Yoke, tie, and sleeve cut-in-one

Basic Patterns

- ▪ The Kimono Sleeve & Fitted Bodice, **pages 8–11**
- ▪ The Kimono Sleeve with Underarm Curve, **page 13**
- ▪ The Long Kimono Sleeve—Fitted, **page 14**

**Drafts
Step 1**

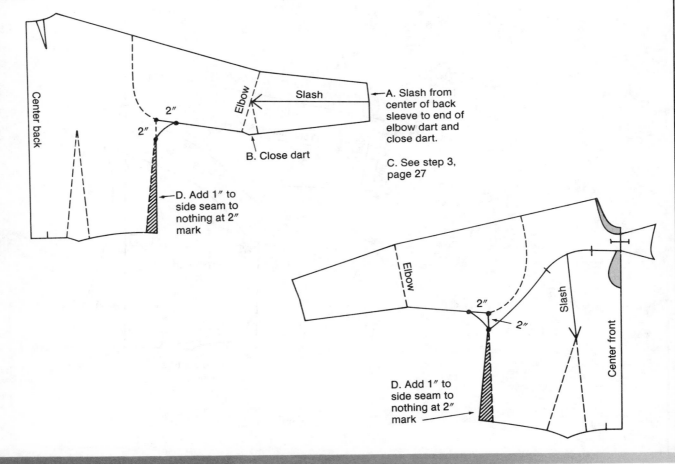

Center back

2″
2″

Elbow

Slash

A. Slash from center of back sleeve to end of elbow dart and close dart.

B. Close dart

C. See step 3, page 27

D. Add 1″ to side seam to nothing at 2″ mark

Elbow

2″
2″

Slash

Center front

D. Add 1″ to side seam to nothing at 2″ mark

Step 2

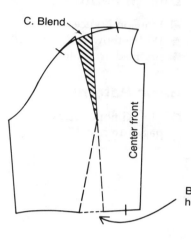

C. Blend

Center front

B. Fold dart
halfway closed

Step 3

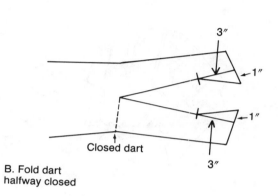

3″

1″

1″

Closed dart

3″

Patterns

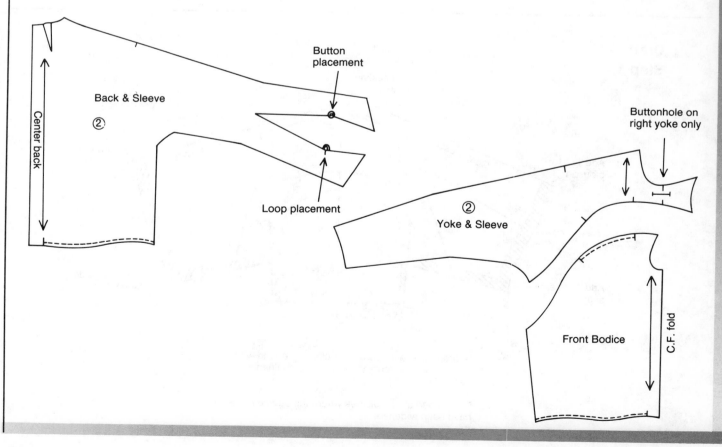

Back & Sleeve

②

Center back

Button
placement

Loop placement

Buttonhole on
right yoke only

②

Yoke & Sleeve

Front Bodice

C.F. fold

Kimono Sleeve with Stylized Armhole

DESIGN VARIATION

Design Features

■ Blouson bodice
■ Wide elbow-length cuffed sleeves
■ Stylized armholes

Basic Patterns

■ The Kimono Sleeve-Bodice in One Piece, **pages 16** and **17**

Draft
Step 1

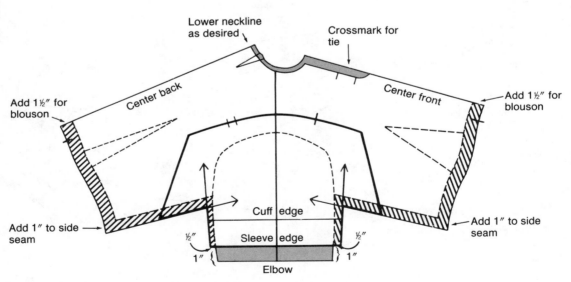

Shorten sleeve 1″ above the elbow line, and widen it ½″ at each underarm. (The sleeve is outlined with a heavy line.)

The striped area indicates where the bodice and sleeve have been widened.

Step 2 Underarm Curve

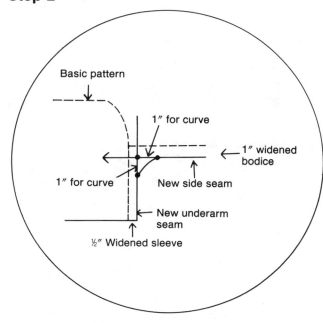

The enlarged view of the underarm shows that an underarm curve has been made 1″ × 1″ (see dots) rather than the standard 2″ × 2″ since the bodice and sleeve have already been widened, and a deeper curve would somewhat restrict arm movement.

Patterns

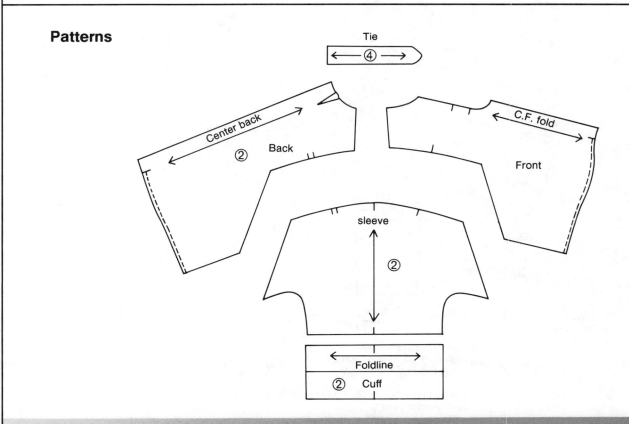

Kimono Sleeve with Square Armhole

DESIGN VARIATION

Design Features

- ■ Tucked front and back waistline
- ■ Three-quarter length kimono sleeves with deep square armholes

Basic Patterns

- ■ The Kimono Sleeve-Bodice in One Piece, **pages 16** and **17.** Pivot waistline dart to side seam.

Draft Step 1

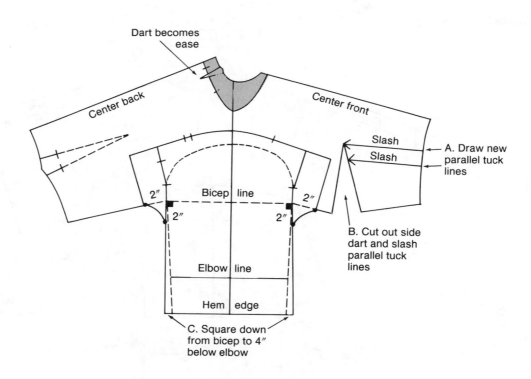

Dart becomes ease

Center back

Center front

Slash

Slash

A. Draw new parallel tuck lines

Bicep line

2″   2″

2″   2″

B. Cut out side dart and slash parallel tuck lines

Elbow line

Hem edge

C. Square down from bicep to 4″ below elbow

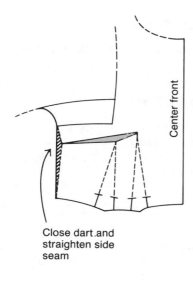

Center front

Close dart.and
straighten side
seam

Step 2. Parallel tucks

A Close the side dart, and push open the slash lines.

B Straighten the side seam.

C Crossmark for tucks.

Patterns

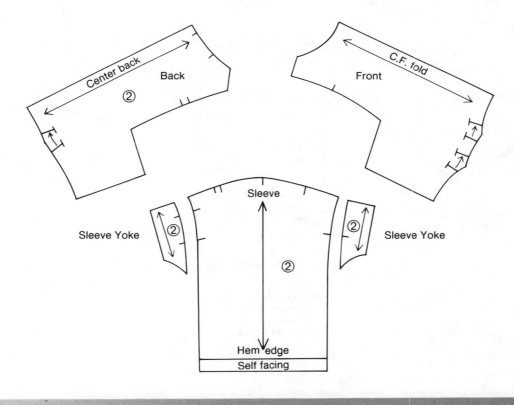

Center back

Back

②

C.F. fold

Front

Sleeve Yoke

②

Sleeve

②

②

Sleeve Yoke

②

Hem edge

Self facing

Kimono Sleeve with Square Armhole

DESIGN VARIATION

Design Features

- Full-length sleeves gathered at the cap and elasticized at the wrist
- Square armhole

Basic Patterns

- The Kimono Sleeve-Bodice in One Piece, **pages 16** and **17**
- The Kimono Sleeve with Underarm Curve, **page 13**

Draft
Step 1

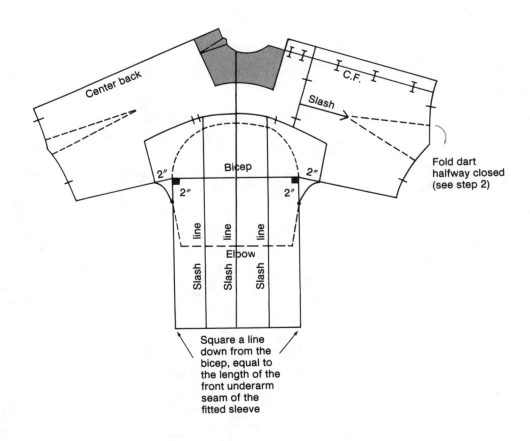

Center back

C.F.

Slash

Bicep

Fold dart halfway closed (see step 2)

2"   2"

2"   2"

Slash line   line   line

Elbow

Slash   Slash   Slash

Square a line down from the bicep, equal to the length of the front underarm seam of the fitted sleeve

Step 2 Gathers at Yoke

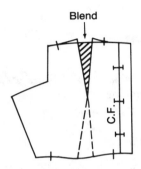

Blend

C.F.

Cut slash line to apex and fold dart halfway closed to obtain gathers at the yokeline.

Step 3 Slashing for Sleeve Fullness

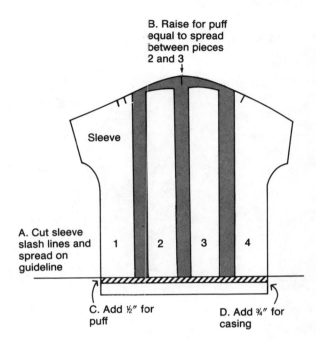

B. Raise for puff equal to spread between pieces 2 and 3

Sleeve

A. Cut sleeve slash lines and spread on guideline

1   2   3   4

C. Add ½" for puff

D. Add ¾" for casing

Patterns

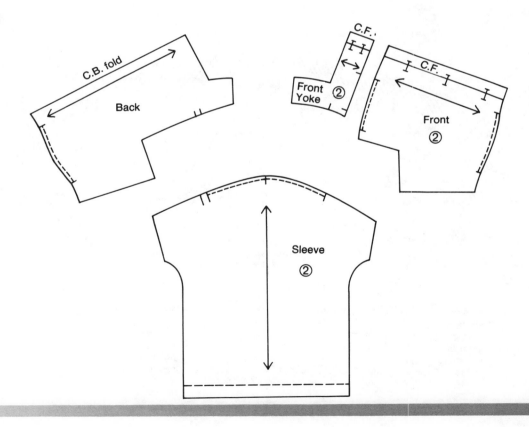

C.B. fold

Back

C.F.

Front Yoke ②

C.F.

Front ②

Sleeve ②

DESIGN VARIATION

Kimono-Raglan Sleeve

Design Features

- ■ Blouson
- ■ Gathers at neckline on front and back
- ■ Snap closings on raglan seam
- ■ Shirtwaist sleeve with cuffs

Basic Patterns

- ■ Kimono-Raglan Bodice, **pages 18** and **19**

**Draft
Step 1**

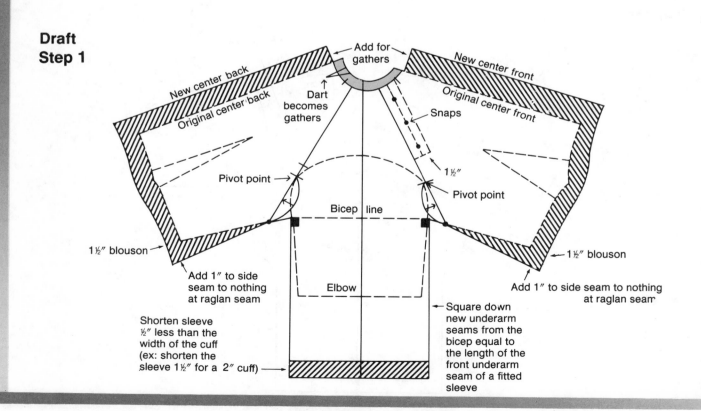

New center back

Original center back

Add for gathers

New center front

Original center front

Dart becomes gathers

Snaps

1½″

Pivot point

Pivot point

Bicep line

1½″ blouson

1½″ blouson

Add 1″ to side seam to nothing at raglan seam

Elbow

Add 1″ to side seam to nothing at raglan seam

Shorten sleeve ½″ less than the width of the cuff (ex: shorten the sleeve 1½″ for a 2″ cuff)

Square down new underarm seams from the bicep equal to the length of the front underarm seam of a fitted sleeve

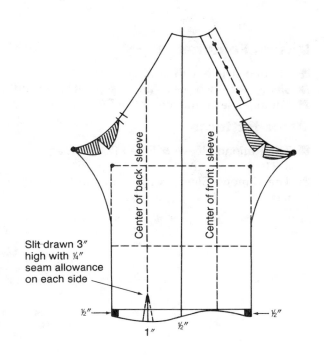

Center of back sleeve

Center of front sleeve

Slit drawn 3″ high with ¼″ seam allowance on each side

½″   ½″

1″   ½″

Step 2. Shirtwaist Sleeve

A Trace the sleeve.

B Follow Step 2, **page 19.**

C Shape new wristline (as shown), smoothly connecting each measurement.

Step 3

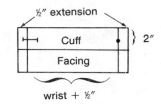

½″ extension

Cuff   } 2″

Facing

wrist + ½″

Patterns

The final patterns have been reduced in scale.

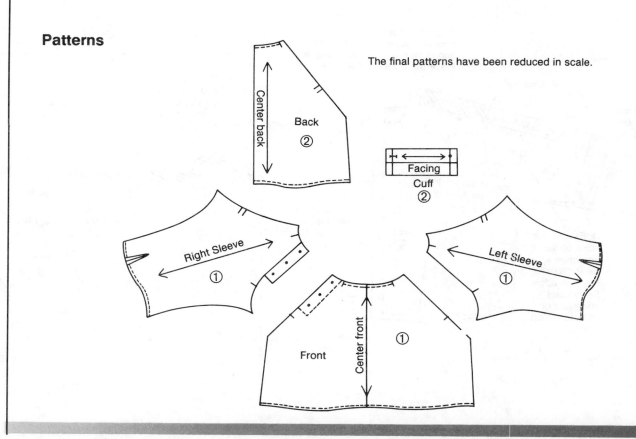

Center back

Back
②

Facing
Cuff
②

Right Sleeve
①

Left Sleeve
①

Center front

Front   ①

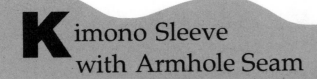

Kimono Sleeve with Armhole Seam

Design on the Dotted Line

Design Features

- Kimono sleeve with armhole seam
- Sleeve with two pleats and a separate split cuff
- Shoulder seam moved to front yoke

Basic Patterns

- The Kimono Sleeve & Fitted Bodice, **pages 8–11**
- The Kimono Sleeve with Armhole Seam, **page 12**

Drafts

Step 1

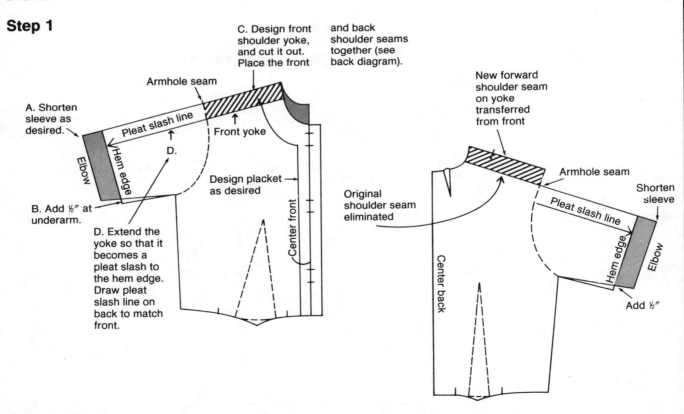

C. Design front shoulder yoke, and cut it out. Place the front and back shoulder seams together (see back diagram).

Armhole seam

A. Shorten sleeve as desired.

Pleat slash line

Front yoke

Elbow

Hem edge

D.

Design placket as desired

Center front

B. Add ½" at underarm.

D. Extend the yoke so that it becomes a pleat slash to the hem edge. Draw pleat slash line on back to match front.

New forward shoulder seam on yoke transferred from front

Armhole seam

Shorten sleeve

Original shoulder seam eliminated

Pleat slash line

Hem edge

Elbow

Center back

Add ½"

Step 2

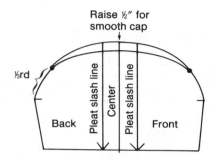

Raise ½" for smooth cap

⅓rd

Back • Pleat slash line • Center • Pleat slash line • Front

A. Trace front and back sleeve section, joining them at their center lines.

B. Raise cap ½" and connect to the last third of the cap front and back (black dots).

Step 4

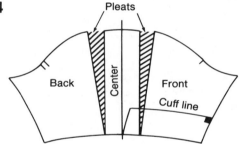

Pleats

Back • Center • Front

Cuff line

A. Slash pleat lines to bicep edge and spread desired amount.

B. Design the split cuff as shown squared at the underarm and then curved parallel to the hem.

Step 3

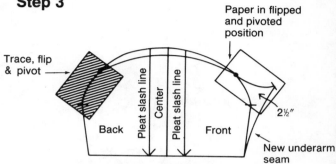

Paper in flipped and pivoted position

Trace, flip & pivot →

Back • Pleat slash line • Center • Pleat slash line • Front

2½"

New underarm seam

A. Trace the last third of the armhole on a separate piece of paper.

B. Flip paper over, touch the last third marks to each other and pivot the tracing up 2½". Draw a gently curved new underarm seam to sleeve edge.

C. Repeat all steps for back. Balance the new underarm seams.

Step 5

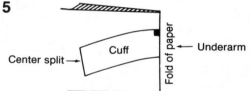

Center split → Cuff ← Underarm

Fold of paper

A. Trace cuff on another piece of paper.

B. Place cuff underarm on a fold of paper and trace.

Patterns

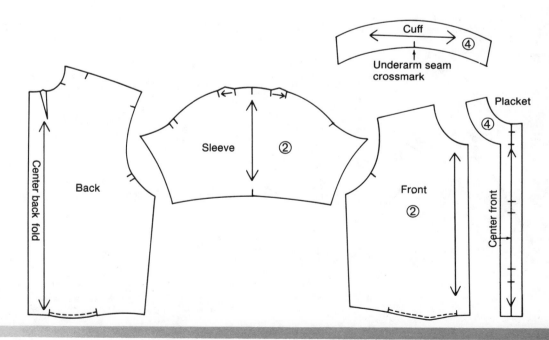

Cuff ④

Underarm seam crossmark

Center back fold

Back

Sleeve ②

Front ②

Placket ④

Center front

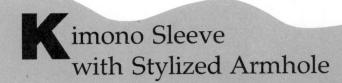

Kimono Sleeve with Stylized Armhole

DESIGN VARIATION

Design Features

- Front-wrapped bodice
- Short kimono sleeves
- Stylized armhole

Basic Patterns

- The Kimono Sleeve-Bodice in One Piece, **pages 16** and **17**

Draft

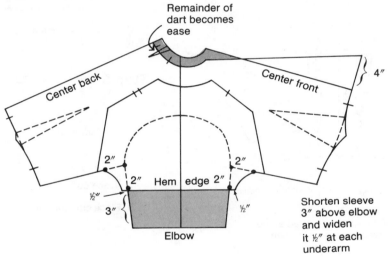

Remainder of dart becomes ease

Center back

Center front

4"

2"

2"

2" Hem edge 2"

2"

½"

½"

3"

Elbow

Shorten sleeve 3" above elbow and widen it ½" at each underarm

Patterns

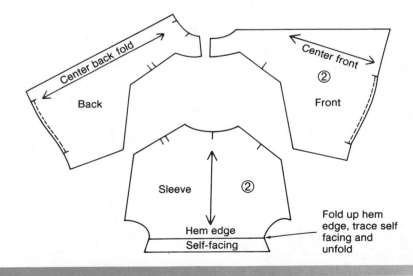

Center back fold

Back

Center front

②

Front

Sleeve

②

Hem edge

Self-facing

Fold up hem edge, trace self facing and unfold

Kimono Sleeve & Hip-Length Pattern

Design Features

■ Boxy kimono that combines a tank top look with an off-the-shoulder neckline
■ Shirtwaist sleeve elasticized at the wrist

Basic Patterns

■ The Kimono Sleeve & Hip-Length Pattern, Boxy Silhouette, **page 20.** Pivot shoulder dart to neckline.
■ The Long Kimono Sleeve—Straight, **page 15**

Drafts

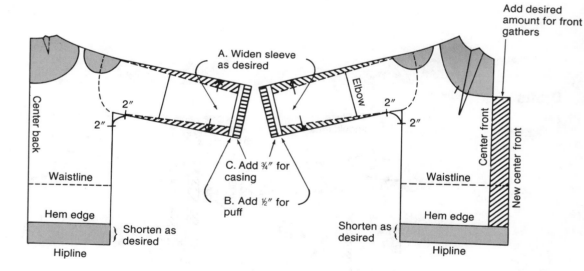

Add desired amount for front gathers

A. Widen sleeve as desired

Center back

2"
2"

Waistline

Hem edge

Shorten as desired

Hipline

C. Add ¾" for casing

B. Add ½" for puff

Elbow

2"
2"

Center front

New center front

Waistline

Hem edge

Shorten as desired

Hipline

Patterns

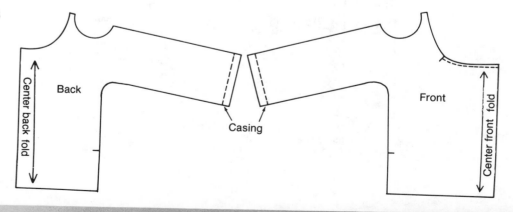

Center back fold

Back

Casing

Front

Center front fold

Kimono Sleeve & Hip-Length Pattern

A Clean Sweep

Design Features

- ■ Flared pullover top
- ■ Short kimono sleeves
- ■ Welt pockets

Basic Patterns

- ■ The Kimono Sleeve & Hip-Length Pattern, Flared Silhouette, **page 21**

Drafts

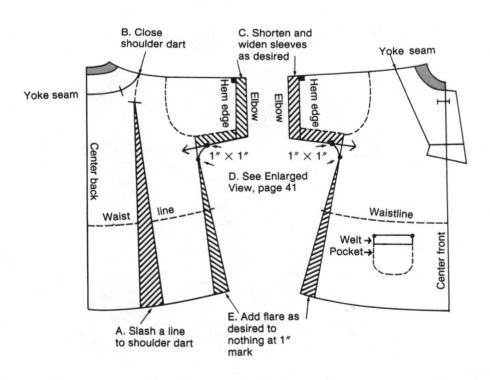

B. Close shoulder dart

C. Shorten and widen sleeves as desired

Yoke seam

Yoke seam

Hem edge

Elbow

Elbow

Hem edge

Center back

1" × 1"

1" × 1"

D. See Enlarged View, page 41

Waist line

Waistline

Welt → Pocket →

Center front

A. Slash a line to shoulder dart

E. Add flare as desired to nothing at 1" mark

Enlarged view of underarm curve: The underarm curve has been made 1″ × 1″ rather than the standard 2″ × 2″, because the sleeve has been widened, and a 2″ × 2″ curve would somewhat restrict arm movement.

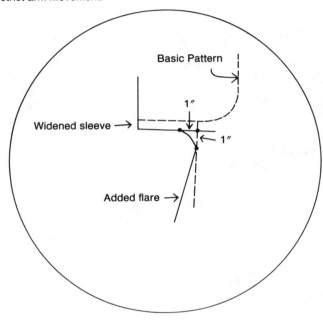

Patterns

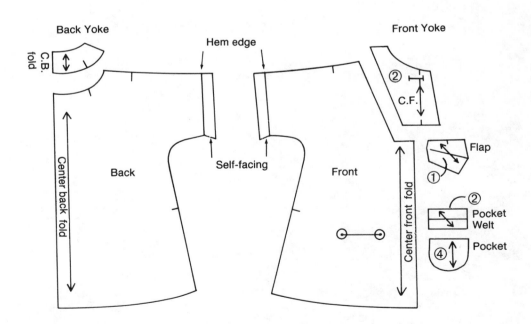

T*wo*

The Dolman Sleeve

Dolman Sleeve & Fitted Bodice

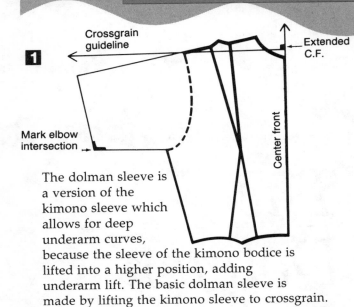

1

Crossgrain guideline

Extended C.F.

Mark elbow intersection

Center front

The dolman sleeve is a version of the kimono sleeve which allows for deep underarm curves, because the sleeve of the kimono bodice is lifted into a higher position, adding underarm lift. The basic dolman sleeve is made by lifting the kimono sleeve to crossgrain.

A Trace only bodice of front fitted, two-dart kimono bodice (dark lines). Mark lower elbow intersection.

B Square a crossgrain guideline from an extended center front through the shoulder/ armhole intersection.

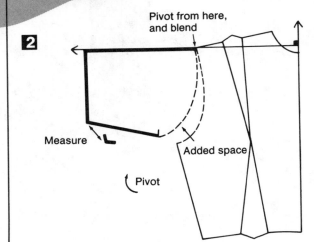

2

Pivot from here, and blend

Measure

Added space

Pivot

C Pivot the kimono upward from the shoulder until the sleeve's overarm lies on the guideline. Trace the sleeve. (The diagram shows the added underarm space which will allow for deeper curves.) Blend the pivot point.

D Measure the distance from the original elbow intersection to the pivoted elbow intersection.

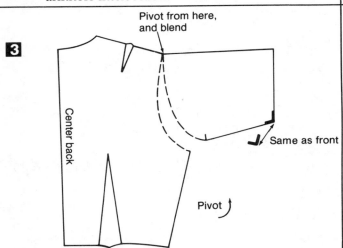

3

Pivot from here, and blend

Center back

Same as front

Pivot

E To obtain matching lift on the back bodice, trace only the bodice section of the back kimono. Mark the lower elbow intersection.

F Pivot the kimono upward from the shoulder until the distance between the marked and the raised elbows exactly matches the distance measured from the front. Trace the sleeve, and blend the pivot point. (The back sleeve may not be on crossgrain. The matching elbow lift is the only guide needed on the back.)

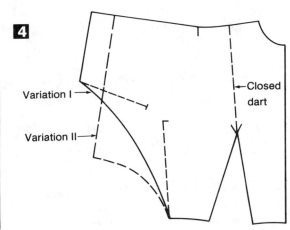

4

Variation I

Variation II

Closed dart

The shoulder dart may be pivoted into the waistline, if desired. Whether or not this is done, the front and back will have exactly matching lifted underarms. Any underarm shape desired may be drawn on the front and then transferred to the back.

Illustrated are just two design variations from an infinite number of possibilities of shortened, lengthened or widened dolman sleeves.

. . . in Your Allowance

5

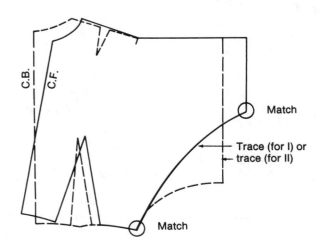

Match

Trace (for I) or
trace (for II)

Match

G To transfer the new underarm silhouette to the back, flip the front bodice over onto the back, matching only the original side seam/ waistline intersections, and the lifted elbow intersections. No other parts of the bodice need to be matched.

H Trace the new underarm silhouette from the front onto the back. Separate the bodices and trace the front and back patterns.

Patterns

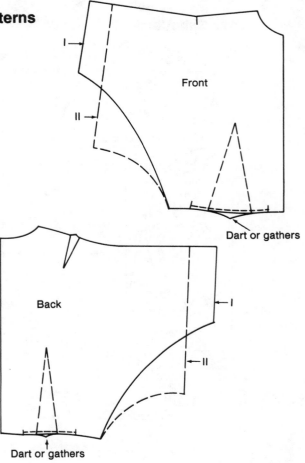

Front

Dart or gathers

Back

Dart or gathers

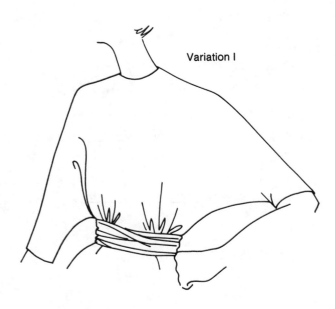

Variation I

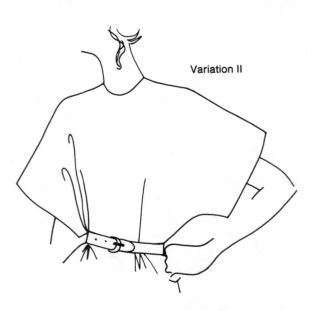

Variation II

Dolman Sleeve & Hip-Length Pattern

Boxy Silhouette

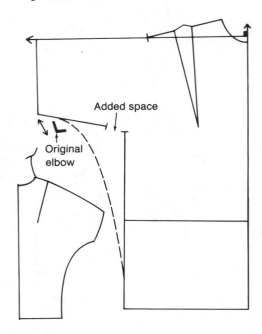

Added space

Original elbow

The dolman sleeve can be created on any hip-length pattern by using one of the kimono sleeve and hip-length patterns, **pages 20** and **21.**

Follow instructions for Dolman Sleeve & Fitted Bodice, **pages 44** and **45**, for the fitted, semi-fitted, and boxy silhouettes.

The broken lines in the diagrams on these pages indicate various underarm silhouettes.

Fitted Silhouette

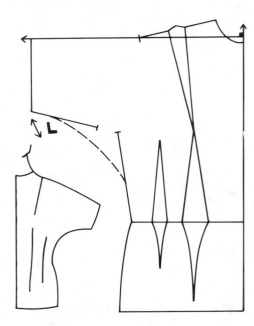

Semi-Fitted Silhouette

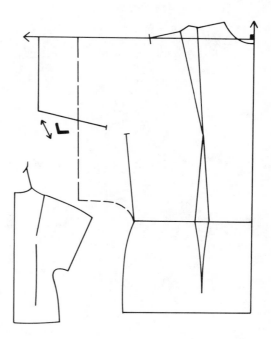

Flared Silhouette

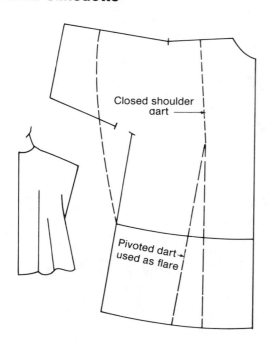

Closed shoulder dart

Pivoted dart used as flare

The dolman flared hip-length pattern is created from the boxy pattern with a dolman sleeve. Close the shoulder dart into flare at the hem. The sleeve will rise above crossgrain, since it begins on crossgrain on the boxy pattern, but the added space at the underarm is the same as on the boxy pattern. For back flare, see **page 40.**

Design
Variations

Dolman Sleeve

DESIGN VARIATION

Design Features

- Elbow-length dolman sleeves with unsewn overarm
- Bateau neckline
- Fitted midriff

Basic Patterns

- The Dolman Sleeve, **pages 44** and **45**

Drafts

Step 1

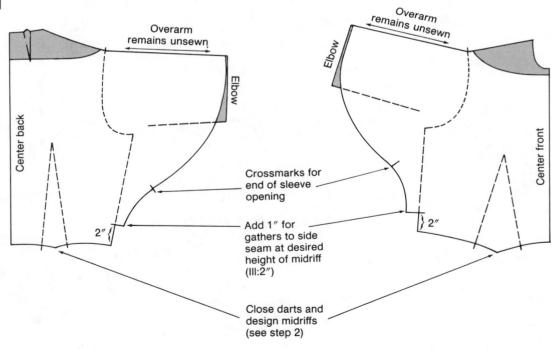

Overarm remains unsewn

Elbow

Center back

Overarm remains unsewn

Elbow

Center front

Crossmarks for end of sleeve opening

2″

Add 1″ for gathers to side seam at desired height of midriff (III:2″)

2″

Close darts and design midriffs (see step 2)

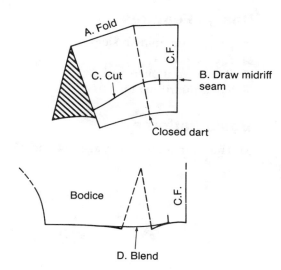

Step 2. Fitted Midriff Seams

A Fold under front bodice across apex of dart.

B Fold waistline dart closed and design a midriff seam to the side seam crossmark made in Step 1. Place a crossmark to indicate gathers.

C Cut through midriff seam.

D The midriff section will remain closed. Only the bodice section will re-open. Blend a smooth line for gathers across the open dart in the bodice section.

E Repeat for the back midriff.

DESIGN VARIATION

Patterns

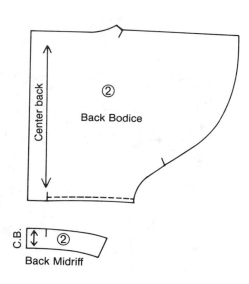

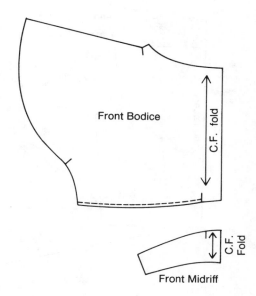

Dolman Sleeve

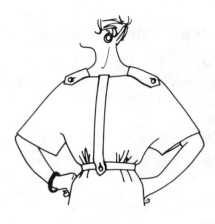

Design Features

- Short wide dolman sleeves
- Shoulder tabs
- Center front overband
- Fitted midriff band

Basic Patterns

- The Dolman Sleeve, **pages 44** and **45**

Drafts

Step 1

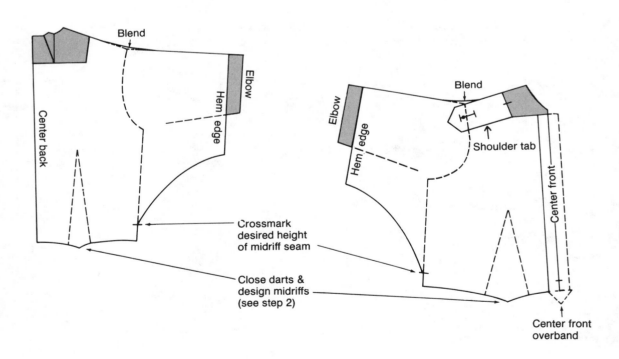

Blend

Elbow

Hem edge

Center back

Elbow

Hem edge

Blend

Shoulder tab

Center front

Crossmark desired height of midriff seam

Close darts & design midriffs (see step 2)

Center front overband

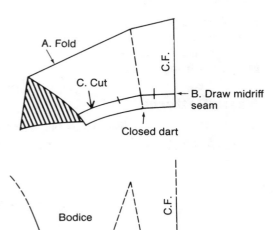

Step 2. Fitted Midriff Seams

A Fold under front bodice across apex of dart.

B Fold waistline dart closed and design a midriff seam to the side seam crossmark made in Step 1. Indicate crossmarks for gathers.

C Cut through midriff seam.

D The midriff section will remain closed. Only the bodice section will open. Blend a smooth line for gathers across the open dart in the bodice section.

E Repeat for back midriff.

Patterns

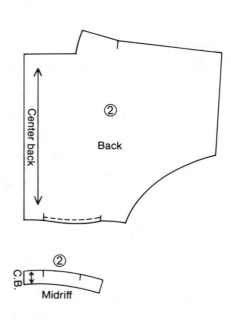

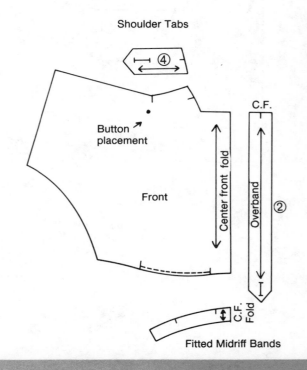

Dolman Sleeve

DESIGN VARIATION

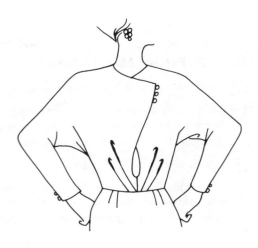

Design Features

■ Dolman sleeve bodice with asymmetrical front closing
■ Center front keyhole design
■ Tucked front and back waistline

Basic Patterns

■ The Dolman Sleeve, **pages 44** and **45,** based on Long Kimono Sleeve—Fitted, **page 14**

Drafts

Step 1

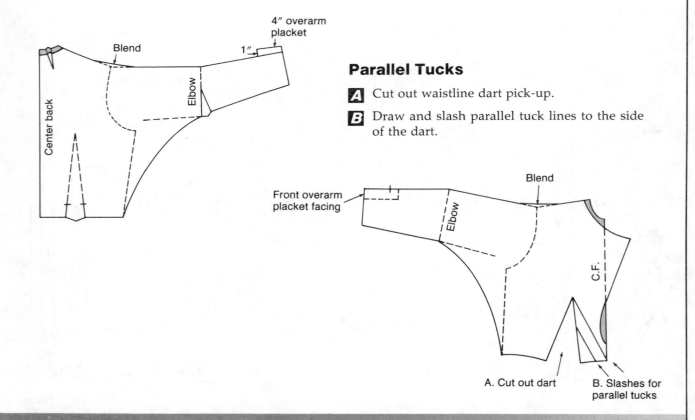

Parallel Tucks

A Cut out waistline dart pick-up.

B Draw and slash parallel tuck lines to the side of the dart.

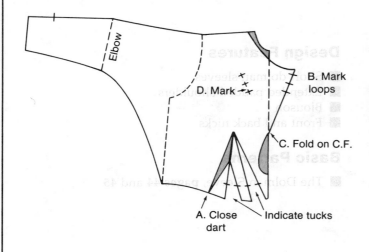

Step 2

A Close dart, and push open the slash lines. Indicate tucks.

B Mark loop locations on overlap.

C Fold on center front and . . .

D . . . transfer those marks onto the bodice for button locations on the left bodice.

DESIGN VARIATION

Patterns

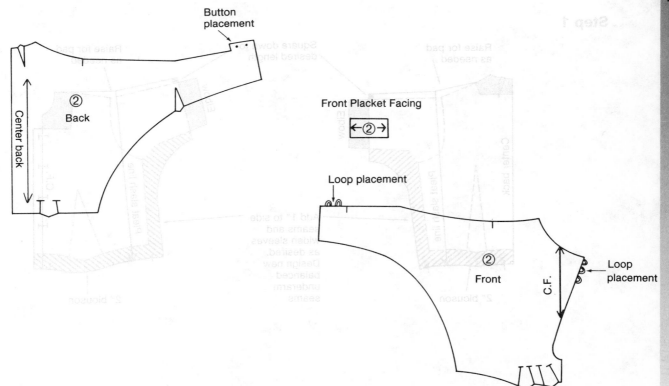

Dolman Sleeve

Design Features

- Short dolman sleeves
- Extended padded shoulders
- Blouson
- Front and back tucks

Basic Patterns

- The Dolman Sleeve, **pages 44** and **45**

Drafts

Step 1

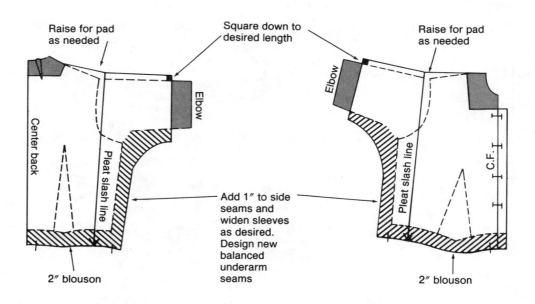

Raise for pad as needed

Square down to desired length

Raise for pad as needed

Elbow

Elbow

Center back

Pleat slash line

Pleat slash line

C.F.

Add 1″ to side seams and widen sleeves as desired. Design new balanced underarm seams

2″ blouson

2″ blouson

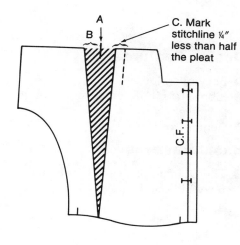

C. Mark stitchline ¼″ less than half the pleat

Step 2. Shoulder Tucks

A Slash pleat line to waistline and spread desired amount for pleat inlay.

B Measure one-half of the pleat.

C For the top-stitching line measure in from the pleat edge ¼″ less than one-half of the pleat.

D Repeat steps for back, spreading the same amount for the back pleat as for the front pleat.

Patterns

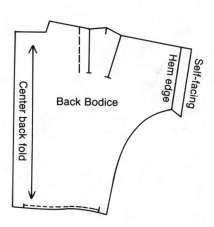

Center back fold

Back Bodice

Hem edge

Self-facing

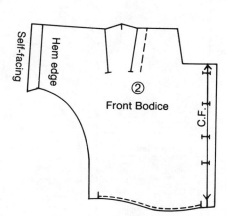

Self-facing

Hem edge

Front Bodice

②

C.F.

Dolman Sleeve

Design Features

- ■ Boxy overblouse
- ■ Elbow-length dolman sleeves designed for a cape effect
- ■ Center front dart

Basic Patterns

- ■ The Dolman Sleeve & Hip-Length Pattern, Boxy Silhouette, **page 46**

Drafts

Step 1

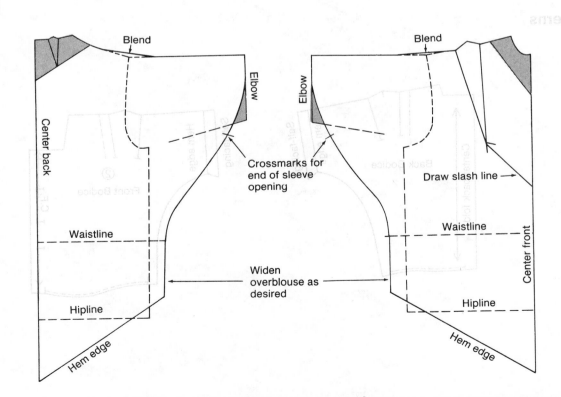

Blend

Blend

Elbow

Elbow

Center back

Crossmarks for end of sleeve opening

Draw slash line →

Waistline

Waistline

Center front

Widen overblouse as desired

Hipline

Hipline

Hem edge

Hem edge

Step 2. Center Front Dart

Cut slash line. Close shoulder dart, transferring it to the center front.

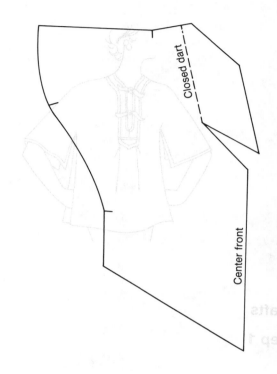

Patterns

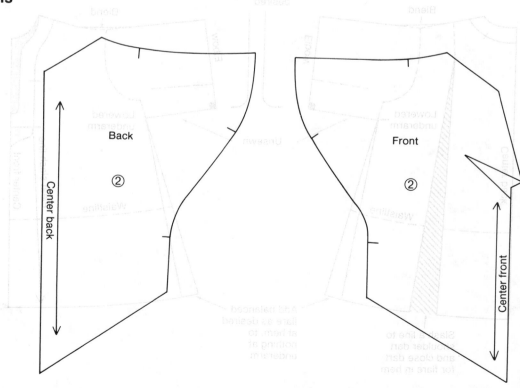

Dolman Sleeve

Design Features

■ Flared pullover top
■ Underarms opened to the side seam
■ Pleats at the center front under a flap

Basic Patterns

■ The Dolman Sleeve & Hip-Length Pattern, Flared Silhouette, **page 47**

Drafts

Step 1

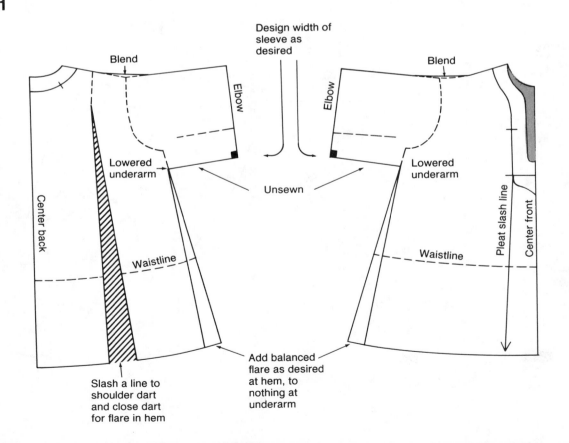

Blend

Design width of sleeve as desired

Blend

Elbow

Elbow

Lowered underarm

Unsewn

Lowered underarm

Center back

Waistline

Waistline

Pleat slash line

Center front

Slash a line to shoulder dart and close dart for flare in hem

Add balanced flare as desired at hem, to nothing at underarm

Step 2. Pleat & Side Pocket

A Slash pleat line and spread amount desired.

B Plan pocket. Crossmark pocket placement on front and back side seams.

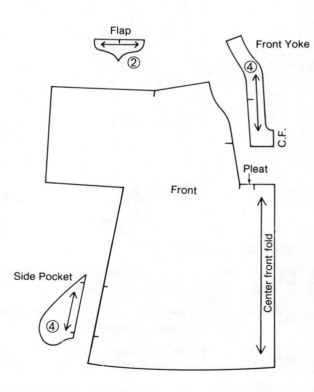

Patterns

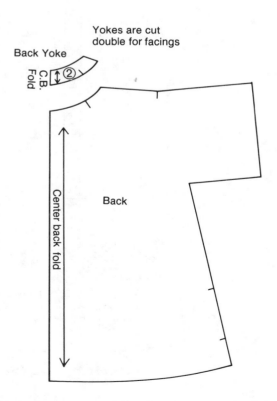

Dolman Sleeve

DESIGN VARIATION

Design Features

- Boxy overblouse
- Short dolman sleeves with overarm slits

Basic Patterns

- The Dolman Sleeve & Hip-Length Pattern, Boxy Silhouette, **page 46**

Drafts

Step 1

Design a lowered neckline, front and back, with a minimum of a 24″ circumference (including the length of the back slit) to allow the blouse to go over the head

Blend — Sleeve opening — Blend

Yoke seam →

Elbow — Sleeve edge — Sleeve edge — Elbow

← Yoke seam

Shorten and widen sleeve as desired

Center back — Slash line — Slash line — Center front

Casing at waistline

Draw the front and back slash lines after designing the yokes as described in step 2

Step 2. Yokes

A Fold under front draft across the apex of the dart. Fold the shoulder dart closed.

B Design a new neckline and a yoke seam, and crossmark to indicate gathers.

C Cut through the yoke seam. Design the back yoke seam on the back bodice and cut through that yoke seam.

New neckline
B. Yoke seam

C. Cut

C.F.

A. Closed dart

Step 3. Gathers

A Separate the yoke from the bodice.

B Cut through the slash line drawn in Step 1, and spread the bodice sections as desired on a hem guideline. The dart is absorbed into the gathers at the yoke seam.

C Blend a new yoke seam from the shoulder seam to center front.

D Repeat for the back bodice.

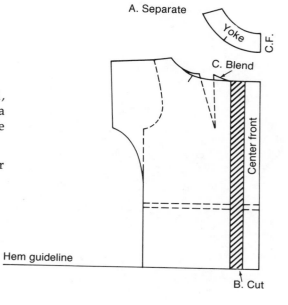

Patterns

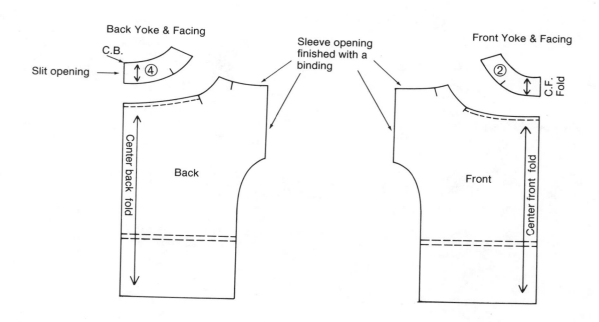

hree

The Batwing Sleeve

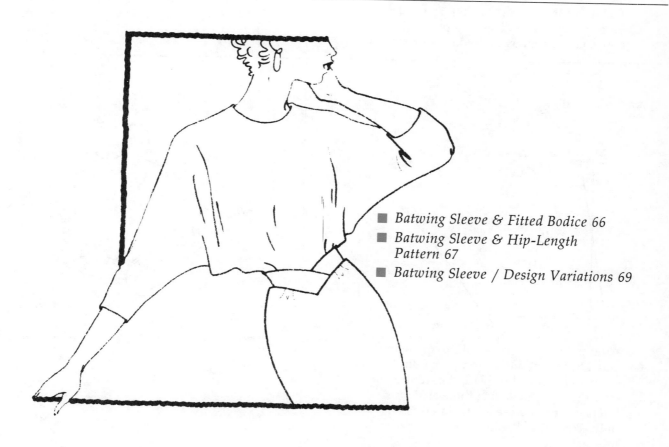

Batwing Sleeve & Fitted Bodice

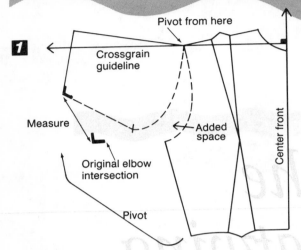

1

Pivot from here

Crossgrain
guideline

Measure

Original elbow
intersection

Added
space

Center front

Pivot

The Batwing sleeve is considered a variation
of the Dolman because its overarm is raised
higher than crossgrain. Because of this higher
lift, more drapery develops under the arm as
it is lowered, due to the extra-long underarm
seam.

Follow all the instructions for The Dolman
Sleeve, **pages 44** and **45,** except lift the sleeve
above crossgrain, as desired.

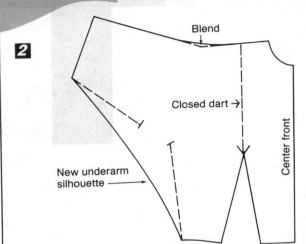

2

Blend

Closed dart →

New underarm
silhouette →

Center front

At this point, the shoulder dart may be
pivoted into the waistline. One possible
underarm silhouette for the Batwing sleeve is
illustrated here. The sleeve can be shortened
or lengthened, widened, etc. Whatever
silhouette is designed, it should be created on
the front bodice first, and then transferred to
the lifted back bodice, as shown in Step 3.

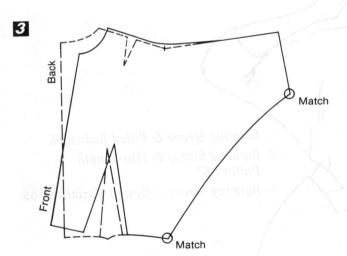

3

Back

Front

Match

Match

After pivoting the back sleeve up an amount
equal to the lift of the front, according to the
Dolman instructions, place the front bodice
over the back, matching the waist
intersections and the elbow intersections
only. Trace the silhouette from the front to
the back.

Batwing Sleeve & Hip-Length Pattern

Bats in Your Belt-Free

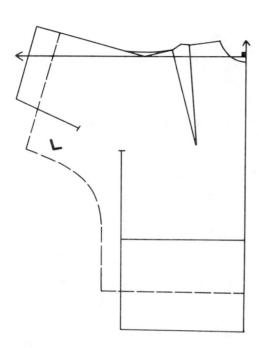

Boxy Silhouette

Semi-Fitted Silhouette

Flared Silhouette

The Batwing sleeve can be created on any kimono sleeve and hip-length pattern (see **pages 20** and **21**). Apply the steps discussed on **page 66** for the Batwing sleeve to the hip-length pattern desired.

The diagram above illustrates a Batwing sleeve with the boxy silhouette (front view); a possible design variation is indicated by broken lines.

Illustrated at the right are Batwing sleeve variations using the boxy, semi-fit and flare silhouettes.

Design
Variations

Batwing Sleeve

DESIGN VARIATION

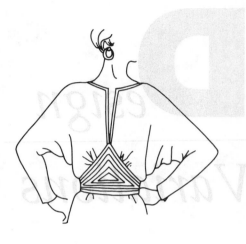

Design Features

■ Batwing sleeve fitted below the elbow with wrist opening in the underarm seam
■ Midriff with top-stitching detail

Basic Patterns

■ The Batwing Sleeve & Fitted Bodice, **page 66**
■ The Long Kimono Sleeve—Fitted, **page 14**

Drafts

Step 1

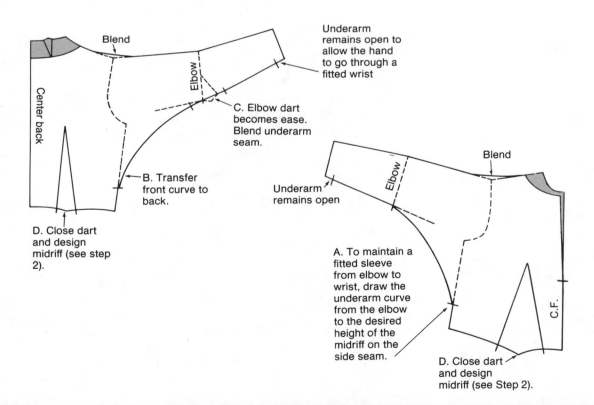

Blend

Underarm remains open to allow the hand to go through a fitted wrist

Elbow

Center back

C. Elbow dart becomes ease. Blend underarm seam.

B. Transfer front curve to back.

D. Close dart and design midriff (see step 2).

Underarm remains open

Elbow

Blend

A. To maintain a fitted sleeve from elbow to wrist, draw the underarm curve from the elbow to the desired height of the midriff on the side seam.

C.F.

D. Close dart and design midriff (see Step 2).

Step 2. Midriffs

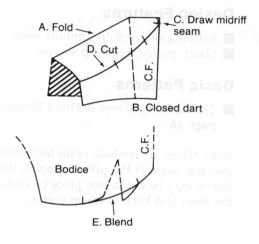

A. Fold
C. Draw midriff seam
D. Cut
C.F.
B. Closed dart

C.F.
Bodice
E. Blend

A Fold under front bodice across the apex of dart.

B Fold waistline dart closed.

C Design a midriff seam to the side seam cross-mark made in Step 1. Indicate crossmarks for gathers.

D Cut through the midriff seam.

E The midriff section will remain closed. Only the bodice section will re-open. Blend a smooth line for gathers across the open dart in the bodice section.

F Repeat for back midriff.

Patterns

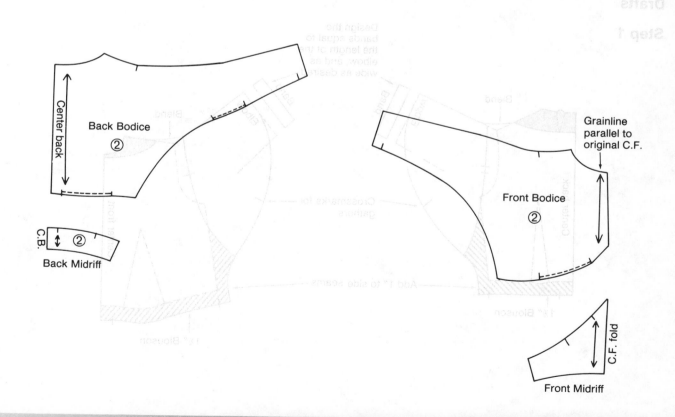

Center back

Back Bodice
②

C.B. ②

Back Midriff

Grainline parallel to original C.F.

Front Bodice
②

C.F. fold

Front Midriff

Batwing Sleeve

DESIGN VARIATION

Design Features

■ Batwing sleeve with armhole seam
■ Short, puffed, push-up sleeves

Basic Patterns

■ The Batwing Sleeve & Fitted Bodice,
page 66

Note: When an armhole seam intersects the overarm seam at the pivoting point, the sleeve may be cut in one piece by matching the front and back overarm seams.

Drafts

Step 1

Design the bands equal to the length of the elbow, and as wide as desired

Blend

Band

Elbow

Band

Elbow

Blend

Center back

Crossmarks for gathers

Center front

Add 1″ to side seams

1½″ Blouson

1½″ Blouson

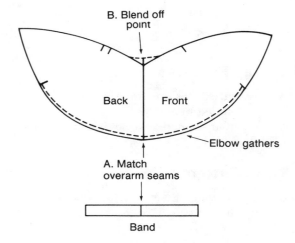

Step 2. Sleeve & Band

Trace the back and front sleeves and bands.

A Join the sleeve overarm seams together, and then the band overarm seams together to form a one-piece sleeve and a one-piece elbow band.

B Blend off point at the overarm of the sleeve cap.

Patterns

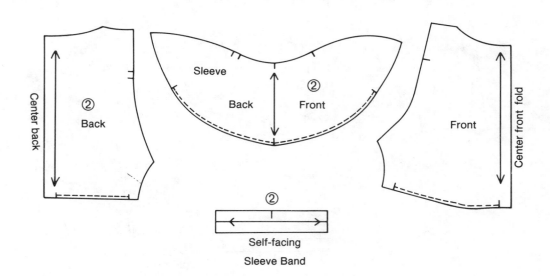

DESIGN VARIATION

Batwing Sleeve

DESIGN VARIATION

Design Features

■ Batwing sleeve in three-quarter length, with banded hem edges

■ Triangular-shaped yoke set into a gathered bodice

Basic Patterns

■ The Batwing Sleeve & Fitted Bodice, **page 66**

Drafts
Step 1

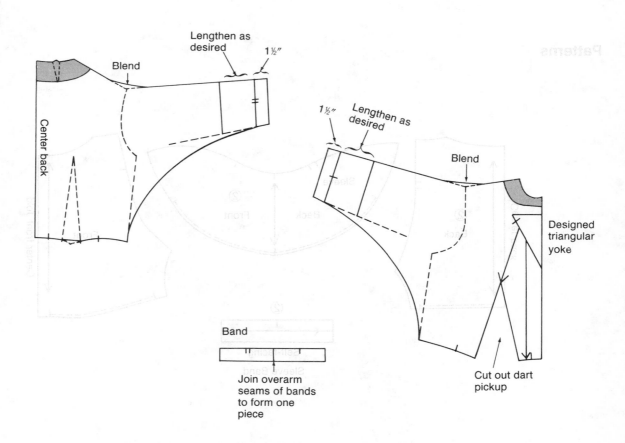

Lengthen as desired

Blend

1½"

Center back

Band

Join overarm seams of bands to form one piece

1½"

Lengthen as desired

Blend

Designed triangular yoke

Cut out dart pickup

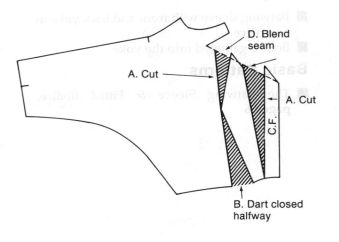

D. Blend seam

A. Cut

A. Cut

C.F.

B. Dart closed halfway

Step 2. Bodice Gathers

A Cut slash lines.

B Close dart halfway.

C Open other slash as desired.

D Blend gathered seam.

Patterns

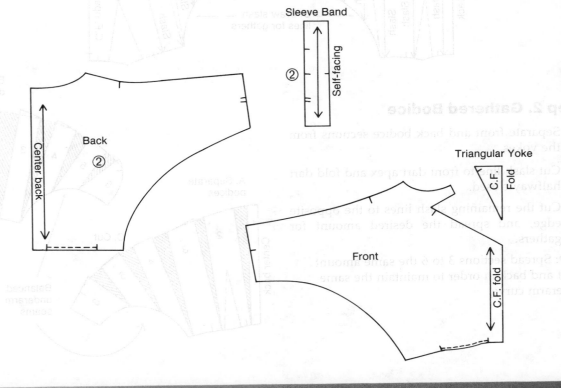

Back

②

Center back

Sleeve Band

②

Self-facing

Triangular Yoke

C.F.

Fold

Front

C.F. fold

Batwing Sleeve

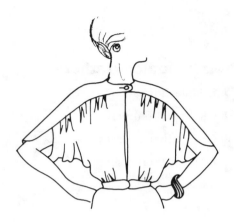

Design Features

■ Batwing sleeve with front and back yoke in one piece
■ Bodice gathered into the yoke

Basic Patterns

■ The Batwing Sleeve & Fitted Bodice, **page 66**

Drafts
Step 1

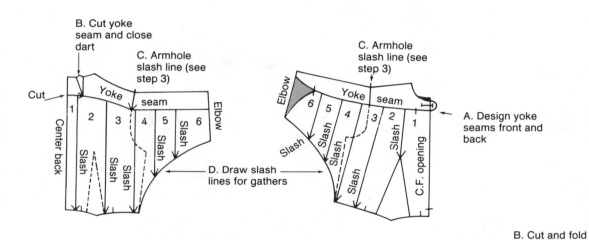

Step 2. Gathered Bodice

A Separate front and back bodice sections from the yokes.

B Cut slash line to front dart apex and fold dart halfway closed.

C Cut the remaining slash lines to the opposite edge, and spread the desired amount for gathers.

Note: Spread sections 3 to 6 the same amount front and back in order to maintain the same underarm curve.

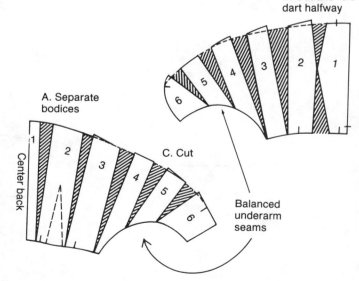

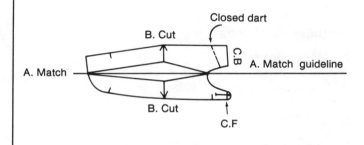

Closed dart

B. Cut

C.B

A. Match — A. Match guideline

A. Match

B. Cut

C.F

Step 3. One-Piece Yoke

A slash on the front and back yoke sections allows the shoulder seam to become a straight line.

A Match the end of the shoulder seams and the neck/shoulder intersections of the front and back yokes to a horizontal guideline.

B Cut the armhole slash lines drawn in Step 1.

C Spread the slash lines until the overarm seams touch the guideline. The space created in this step is used as ease over the shoulder blend yoke lines.

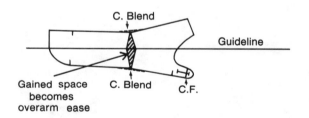

C. Blend

Guideline

Gained space becomes overarm ease

C. Blend

C.F.

Patterns

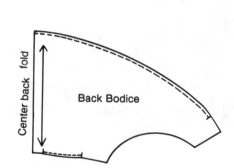

Center back fold

Back Bodice

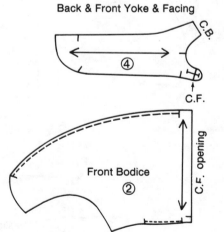

Back & Front Yoke & Facing

C.B.

④

C.F.

Front Bodice
②

C.F. opening

Batwing Sleeve & Hip-Length Pattern

Design Features

- Boxy pullover blouse
- Short batwing sleeve with stylized armhole
- Front and back bodice yokes

Basic Patterns

- The Batwing Sleeve & Hip-Length Pattern—Boxy Silhouette, **page 67**

Drafts

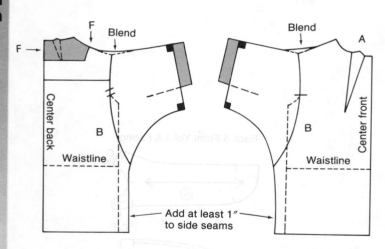

F   Blend   Blend   A

Center back

Center front

Waistline   Waistline

B   B

Add at least 1″ to side seams

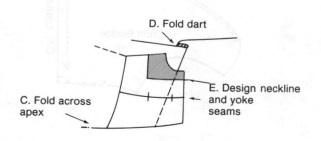

D. Fold dart

C. Fold across apex

E. Design neckline and yoke seams

Step 1

A Pivot front shoulder dart to neckline to clear shoulder area for design.

B Design armhole seams and indicate crossmarks.

Note: See detailed diagram of the front bodice for C, D and E.

C Fold under the front bodice across the apex of the dart.

D Fold dart closed.

E Design the front neckline and yoke seams. Indicate crossmarks for gathers. Cut through the yoke seam, and leave the dart folded in the yoke. Unfold the dart in the bodice, and blend between the crossmarks for gathers.

F Design the neckline and yoke seams on the back bodice to match the seamlines on the front.

Patterns

Back Yoke & Self-Facing
Cut 2

Front Yoke & Self-Facing
Cut 2

C. B. fold

C.F. Fold

Back Sleeve ②

Front Sleeve ②

Center back fold

Back Bodice

Center front fold

Front Bodice

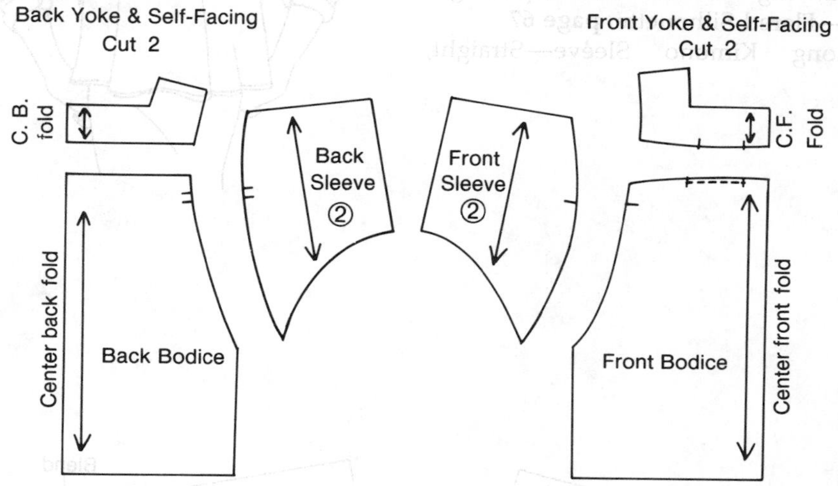

Batwing Sleeve & Hip-Length Pattern

Design Features

- Long straight, push-up batwing sleeve
- Flared, pullover top
- Back neckline slit with loop and button closure

Basic Patterns

- The Batwing Sleeve & Hip-Length Pattern—Flared Silhouette, **page 67**
- The Long Kimono Sleeve—Straight, **page 15**

Drafts

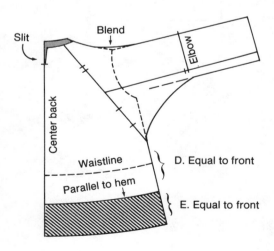

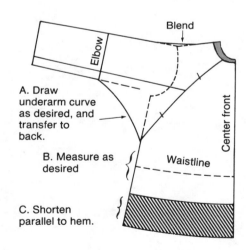

A. Draw underarm curve as desired, and transfer to back.

B. Measure as desired

C. Shorten parallel to hem.

D. Equal to front

E. Equal to front

Patterns

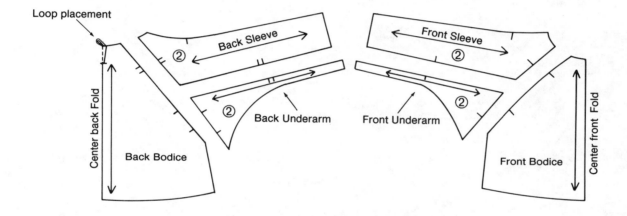

Loop placement

Back Sleeve

②

Center back Fold

Back Bodice

②

Back Underarm

Front Sleeve

②

②

Front Underarm

Front Bodice

Center front Fold

Patterns

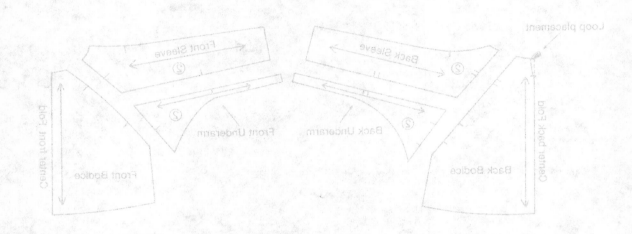

Front Sleeve

Back Sleeve

Front Underarm

Back Underarm

Center front Fold

Center back Fold

Front Bodice

Back Bodice

Loop placement

Four

The Gusset Sleeve

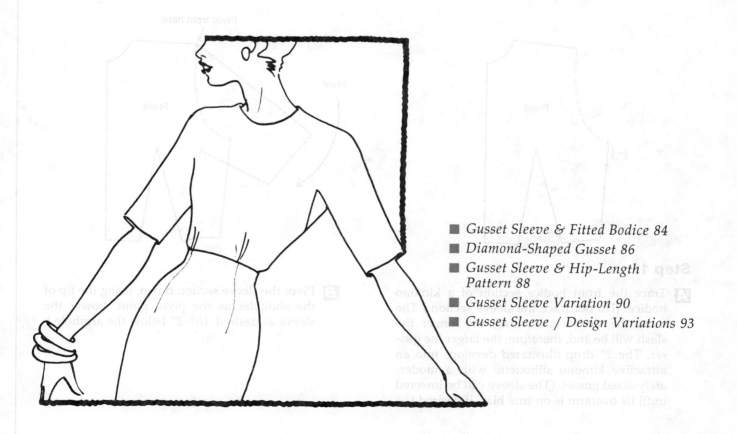

Gusset Sleeve & Fitted Bodice

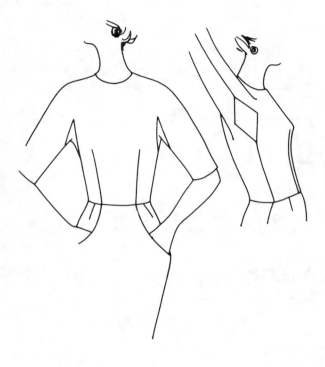

The gusset sleeve is a variation of the kimono in that the sleeve is lowered from the kimono position. This lowered position creates a downward silhouette that restricts the lifting of the arm. The bodice must be slashed in order to restore the lift, causing a diamond-shaped opening which is covered with a patch called a gusset. The gusset sleeve has the most lift of any sleeve, while retaining a smoothly fitted underarm. When the arm is lowered, the gusset is hidden under the arm, giving the garment the one-piece look of the kimono sleeve combined with the close fit of the set-in sleeve.

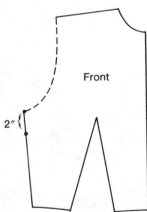

Step 1

A Trace the front bodice section of a kimono bodice. (Do not trace the sleeve section.) The more the sleeve is lowered, the longer the slash will be and, therefore, the larger the gusset. The 2″ drop illustrated develops into an attractive kimono silhouette with a moderately-sized gusset. (The sleeve can be lowered until its overarm is on true bias, if desired.)

B Pivot the sleeve section down, using the tip of the shoulder as the pivot point. Lower the sleeve as desired. (*Ill:* 2″ below the armhole.)

... But An Ace in the Hole

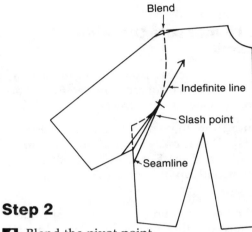

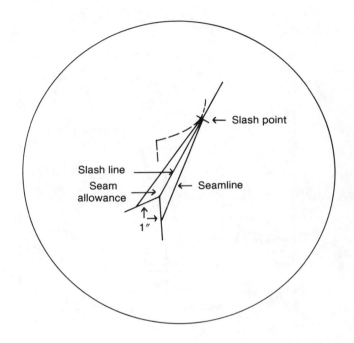

Step 2

A Blend the pivot point.

B Draw an indefinite line up from the underarm intersection that just touches the armhole.

C Mark the point where the indefinite line and the underarm touch as the slash point, which ends the slash line.

D From 1″ down the underarm seam, and from 1″ down the side seam, draw seamlines to the slash point. The space between the slash line and the seamlines is seam allowance (see inset).

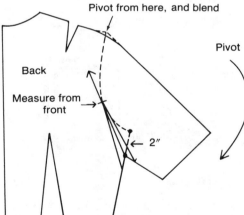

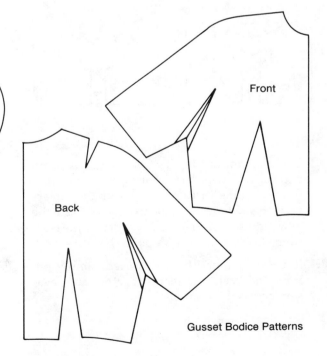

Gusset Bodice Patterns

Step 3

Repeat all steps for the back, with one exception: The slash line from the intersection to the slash point must equal the length of the front slash line. Measure the front slash line, and transfer that distance to the back indefinite line. Mark the back slash point.

The following pages explain the making of the gusset.

Diamond-Shaped Gusset

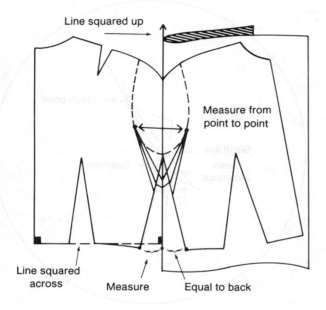

Line squared up

Measure from point to point

Line squared across

Measure

Equal to back

Step 1. To measure the width of the gusset:

A Square a line across from the center back/waistline, and then square a line up from that line to the underarm intersection.

B Measure from the side seam to the vertical line. Repeat that measurement from the front side seam, and mark it. Draw a vertical line from that mark up through the front underarm intersection.

C Fold the front draft under on its vertical guideline. Place the fold next to the back vertical line. The armhole should be clearly "re-created" by this placement.

D Measure across from slash point to slash point.

The width of the armhole becomes the width for the gusset.

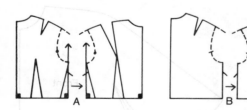

A   B

Step 2

A The diagram in Step 1 is of a one-dart front bodice. If a two-dart front is used, square a new waistline in front and back, and square up a new side seam in the front also. Place the new side seams together in order to measure from slash point to slash point.

B If a boxy kimono bodice is used, simply put front and back side seams together and measure across the armhole.

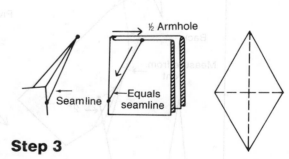

½ Armhole

Seamline

Equals seamline

Step 3

A Fold a piece of paper in fourths. (See Step 4, **page 87** for explanation of why a gusset may be cut on the fold.)

B Measure one-half of the armhole width from the fold, and mark.

C From that mark, measure diagonally toward the fold a distance equal to the gusset seamline (measured from any of the four gusset seamlines on the bodices).

D Cut through the diagonal line, and unfold.

. . . A Girl's Best Friend

Step 4

Since the front and back bodices are balanced, the four gusset seamlines on the bodice will all be the same length. Therefore, the gusset may be cut on folded paper to create a perfectly symmetrical diamond.

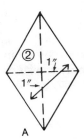 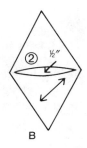  

A   The gusset may be cut on the bias to counter-act the bias grain of the bodice gusset seams. Measure 1″ by 1″ from the center of the creases, and connect the 1″ marks. The out-side seams of the gusset will be on approxi-mate straight and cross grains.

B   For a gusset with more contour, a ½″ wide dart may be created across its width. The dart should be drawn to nothing at each end, stop-ping short of the gusset corners so as not to interfere when these corners are sewn to the bodice.

C   A gusset may have a seam through its center, which makes it easier to insert into the bodice. Cut the original diamond in half, and cut four pieces in fabric.

D   A half-gusset can be contoured by slashing across its width, and then overlapping the upper section ½″ onto the lower section. This gusset gives the best shaping under the arm, as well as it being easier to insert than a one-piece gusset.

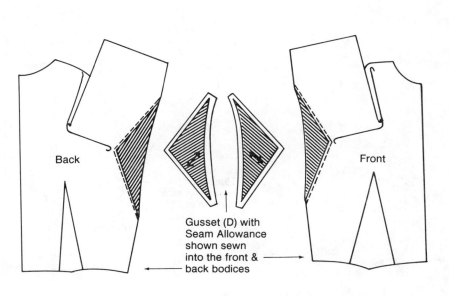

Back

Gusset (D) with Seam Allowance shown sewn into the front & back bodices

Front

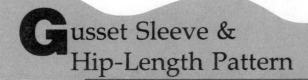

Gusset Sleeve & Hip-Length Pattern

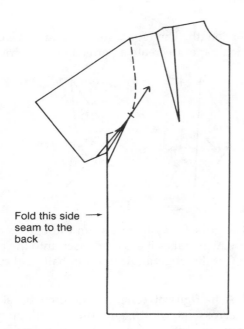

Fold this side
seam to the
back

Boxy Silhouette

The gusset sleeve can be designed on any
hip-length pattern (refer to **pages 20** and **21**
for hip-length pattern). Apply the steps for
the gusset sleeve, **pages 84–87,** to the hip-
length pattern desired.

Semi-Fitted Silhouette

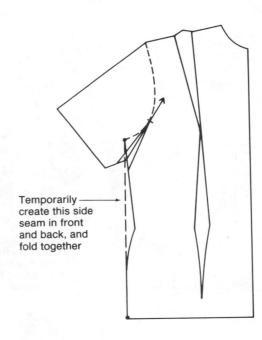

Temporarily
create this side
seam in front
and back, and
fold together

Fitted Silhouette

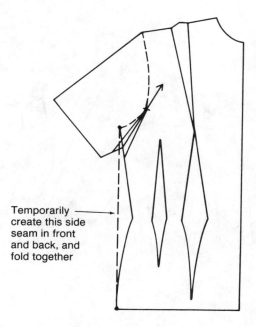

Temporarily create this side seam in front and back, and fold together

Flared Silhouette

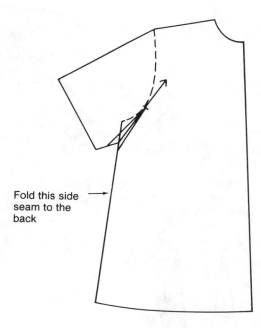

Fold this side seam to the back

Note: The side seam to be folded over to the back is marked in each diagram, to be used in Step 1, **page 86.**

Gusset Sleeve Variation

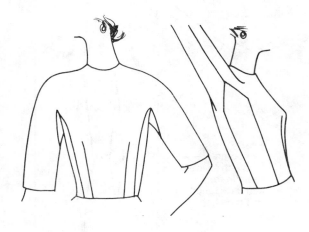

The diamond shape is the minimum-sized gusset that can be used, but a gusset can have an infinite number of shapes. While the slash lines on the bodices and the width of the gusset never change, the seamlines can be planned in any way desired. In this variation, called the House Gusset, only the bodice seamlines are re-designed, but the sleeve seamlines can be changed also, as will be seen in the design variations that follow.

Step 1

A Follow Steps 1, 2 and 3, **pages 84** and **85,** except draw the 1″ seamline on the sleeves only.

B The broken lines are suggested design variation to replace the gusset seamlines on the bodices.

C Cut out the gusset sections (shaded areas), and cut through the slash lines.

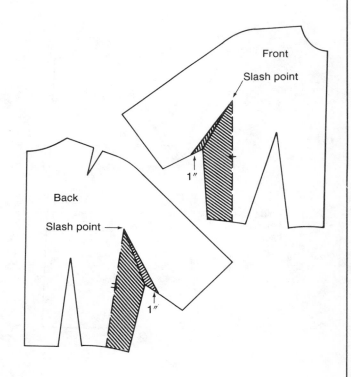

Step 2

Most gusset variations cannot be cut on folded paper, since they are not symmetrical. Therefore, the gusset sections are cut out and spread open individually.

A Draw a long straight line on a piece of paper, and square a shorter line across it. Balance the width of the gusset (Step 1, **page 84**) on the squared line.

B Place the cut gusset sections so that their slash points touch the ends of the balanced width of the gusset. Move the sleeve pieces until they touch the long straight line. Then move the bodice sections until they touch to the long straight line. Trace the outline of the piece for the pattern.

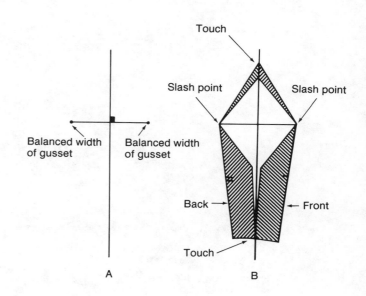

Patterns

(without seam allowance)

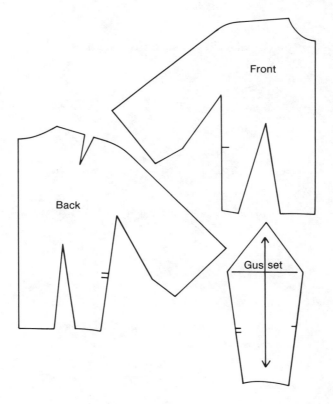

Design

Variations

Gusset Sleeve

Design Features

- Stylized house gusset with seams that join the waistline darts
- Short, puffed, push-up sleeve with wide bands that button at the overarm sleeve slit

Basic Patterns

- The Gusset Sleeve Variation, Step 1, **page 90,** designing the gusset seams to intersect the front and back waistline darts.

Drafts

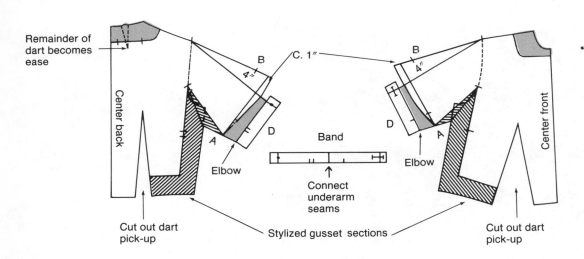

Step 1

A Shorten sleeves as desired.

B Widen sleeves for gathers (*Ill:* 4″). Crossmark overarm seam slit.

C Lengthen sleeve overarms 1″ for puff.

D Design the sleeve bands at the original elbow line, so that they will cause puff when they are pushed up to the wider bicep circumference. Indicate crossmarks.

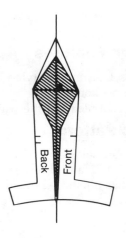

Step 2. Gusset

Trace front and back gusset sections (striped areas in Step 1), and then cut them out.

To complete the stylized gusset, see Step 2, **page 91.**

Patterns

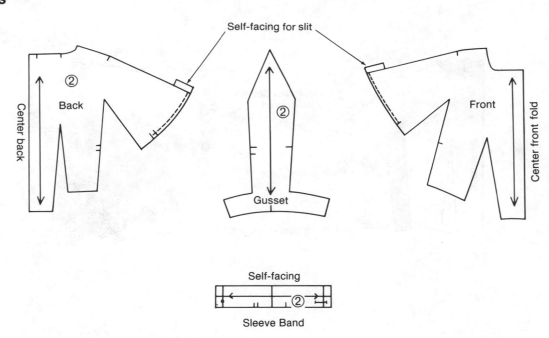

D E S I G N   V A R I A T I O N

Gusset Sleeve

DESIGN VARIATION

Design Features

- Gusset seamline styled into a yoke with welt pockets
- Inverted pleats at the waistline

Basic Patterns

- The Gusset Sleeve Variation, **pages 90–91**, Steps 1, 2 and 3, except design the seamlines as illustrated below.

Drafts

Step 1

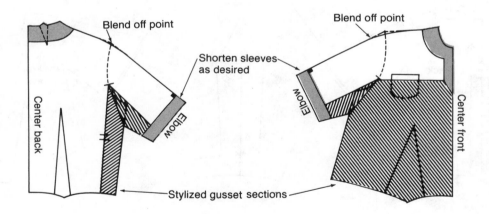

Blend off point

Blend off point

Shorten sleeves as desired

Center back

Elbow

Elbow

Center front

Stylized gusset sections

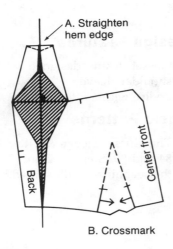

Step 2. Gusset

Trace front and back gusset sections (striped areas, Step 1), and then cut out. To complete gusset, see **page 90,** Step 2.

A Straighten hem edge to avoid an angle that would distort sleeve hem edge.

B Crossmark the dart to change it into a tuck. Fold tuck as indicated by arrows, and true it with a tracing wheel.

DESIGN VARIATION

Patterns

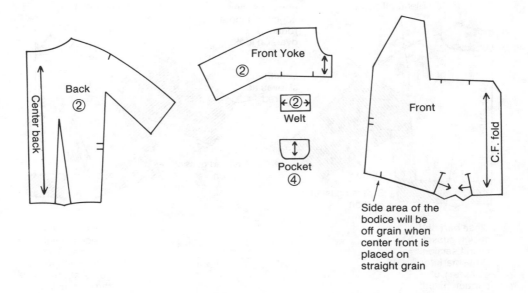

Gusset Sleeve

DESIGN VARIATION

Design Features

■ Gusset seams designed with a dropped-shoulder sleeve
■ Bodice with a fitted midriff

Basic Patterns

■ The Gusset Sleeve & Fitted Bodice, **pages 84** and **85,** Steps 1, 2 and 3, except design the seamlines as illustrated below

Drafts

Step 1

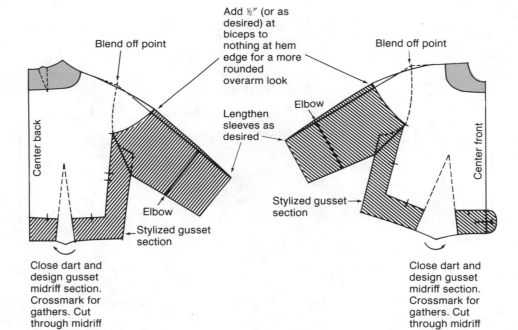

Blend off point

Add ½" (or as desired) at biceps to nothing at hem edge for a more rounded overarm look

Blend off point

Elbow

Lengthen sleeves as desired

Center back

Center front

Elbow

Stylized gusset section

Stylized gusset section

Close dart and design gusset midriff section. Crossmark for gathers. Cut through midriff section. Unfold dart in bodice.

Close dart and design gusset midriff section. Crossmark for gathers. Cut through midriff section. Unfold dart in bodice.

Step 2. Gusset

Trace front and back gusset sections (striped areas, Step 1), and cut them out.

Follow instructions, **page 91,** Step 2.

A Straighten hem edge to avoid an angle, and to allow for a self-facing.

B Fold under on straightened hem edge and trace a portion of the overarm seam. (*Ill*: 2″.) Unfold, and connect the 2″ tracing with a straight line to create a self-facing.

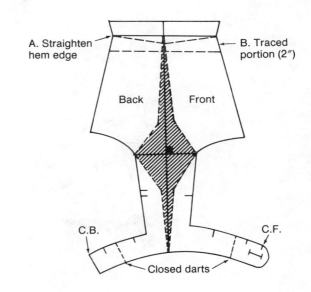

A. Straighten hem edge
B. Traced portion (2″)
Back   Front
C.B.   C.F.
Closed darts

Patterns

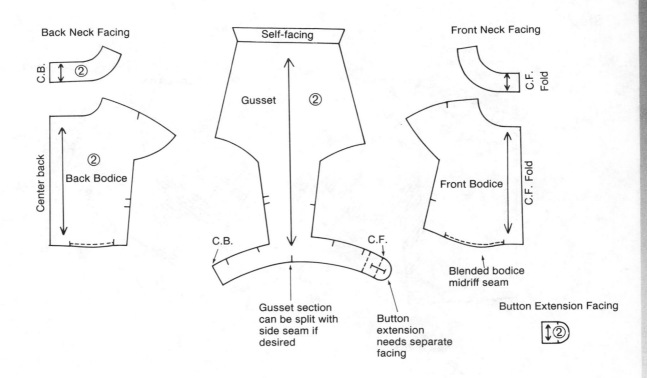

Back Neck Facing
C.B.   ②
Center back   ②   Back Bodice

Self-facing
Gusset   ②
C.B.   C.F.

Gusset section can be split with side seam if desired

Button extension needs separate facing

Front Neck Facing
C.F. Fold   ②

Front Bodice
C.F. Fold

Blended bodice midriff seam

Button Extension Facing
②

Gusset Sleeve

Design Features

- Fitted gusset bodice with sleeve bands created from the gusset seams
- Neckline insert

Basic Patterns

- Pivot the front waistline dart into a french dart. For stylized gusset see The Gusset Sleeve & Fitted Bodice, **pages 84** and **85,** Steps 1, 2 and 3 with this exception:

Draw gusset seamline to the french dart on the front bodice, and on to the sleeve overarm for a sleeve-band effect. Draw the back gusset seams as illustrated, balancing them with the front at the overarm and side seams.

Drafts

Step 1

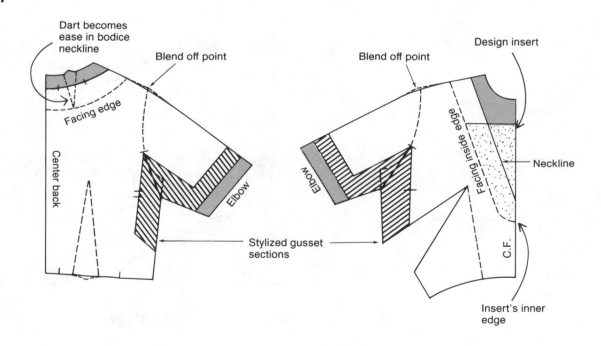

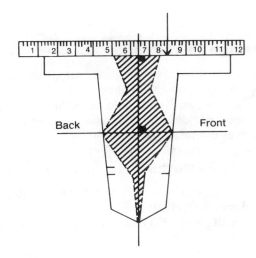

Step 2. Gusset

A Trace front and back gusset sections (striped areas, Step 1), and cut them out. To complete gusset see The Gusset Sleeve, **page 91,** Step 2 with this exception:

To maintain the parallel width of the sleeve band effect, spread the underarm sections until the sleeve hem forms a straight line (refer to diagram for correct placement of ruler).

B Create a self-facing sleeve hem edge (Step 2 B, **page 99**).

DESIGN VARIATION

Patterns

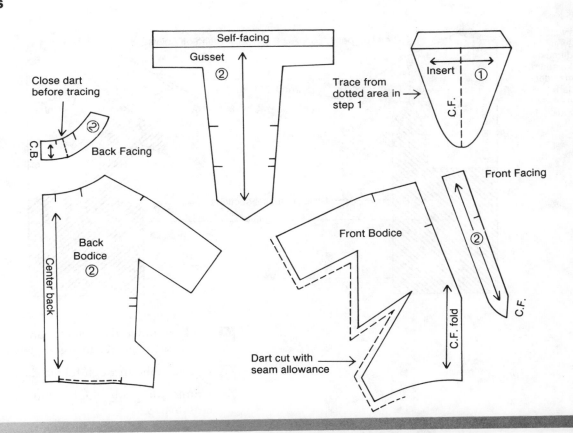

Gusset Sleeve

DESIGN VARIATION

Design Features

■ Pullover blouse with gusset seams that create front and back yokes
■ A side seam with side vent, and a deep open neckline to allow the garment to go over the head

Basic Patterns

■ The Gusset Sleeve & Hip-Length Pattern, **pages 88** and **89**
■ For the stylized gusset design seamlines as illustrated below

Drafts

Fold dart closed and draw lowered neck and yoke seam. The remainder of the dart becomes ease in the bodice.

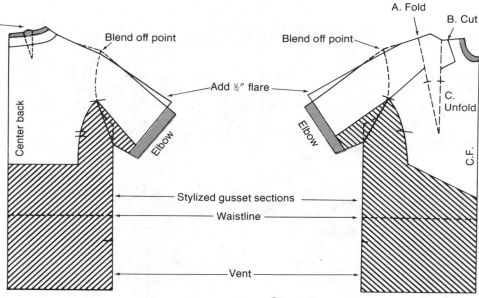

Step 1

A Fold shoulder dart closed and design yoke seam (see **page 62,** enlarged view as a guide).

B Cut yokeline through folded dart.

C Unfold dart in blouse and indicate tuck crossmarks.

Step 2. Gusset

A Trace front and back gusset sections (striped areas, Step 1), and cut them out. Follow Step 2, **page 91.**

B Straighten hem edge to avoid an angle, and to allow for a self-facing (see Step 2 B, **page 99,** for self-facing).

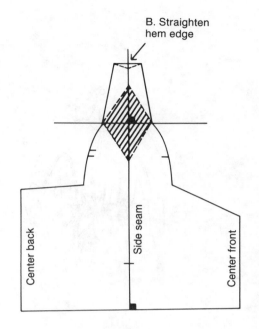

Patterns

The final patterns have been reduced in scale.

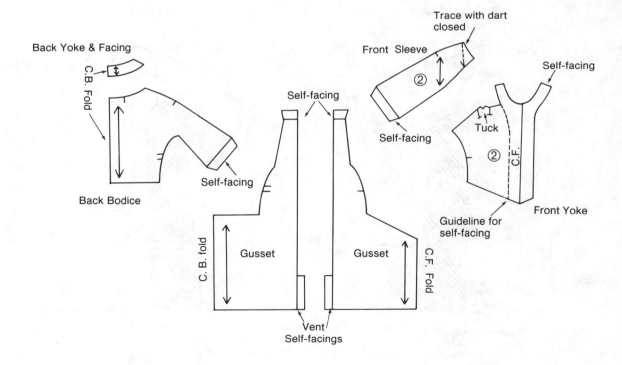

Gusset Sleeve & Hip-Length Pattern

DESIGN VARIATION

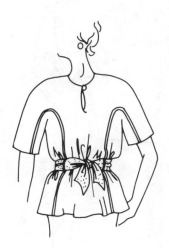

Design Features

■ Gusset is an underarm panel rounded slightly at the top of the armhole slash
■ Flared hip-length overblouse

Basic Patterns

■ The Gusset Sleeve & Hip-Length Pattern— Flared Silhouette, **page 89**

Drafts
Step 1

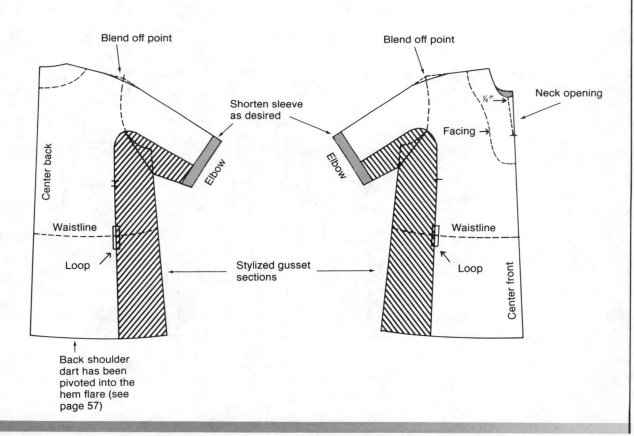

Blend off point

Blend off point

Shorten sleeve as desired

¼"

Neck opening

Facing

Elbow

Elbow

Center back

Waistline

Waistline

Loop

Loop

Stylized gusset sections

Center front

Back shoulder dart has been pivoted into the hem flare (see page 57)

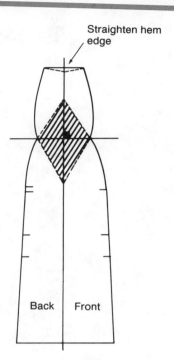

Straighten hem edge

Step 2. Gusset

A Trace front and back gusset sections (striped areas, Step 1), and cut them out.

Follow instructions Step 2, **page 91.**

B Straighten the hem edge to avoid an angle, and to allow for a self-facing (see Step 2 B, **page 99,** for self-facing).

Back   Front

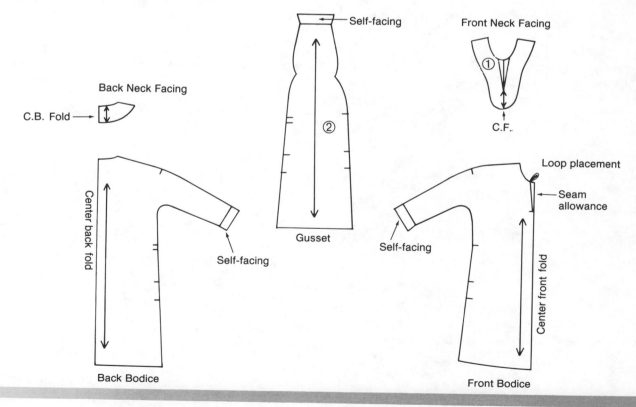

Patterns

The final patterns have been reduced in scale.

Back Neck Facing

C.B. Fold →

Center back fold

Back Bodice

Self-facing

Gusset

Self-facing

Front Neck Facing

C.F.

Loop placement

Seam allowance

Self-facing

Center front fold

Front Bodice

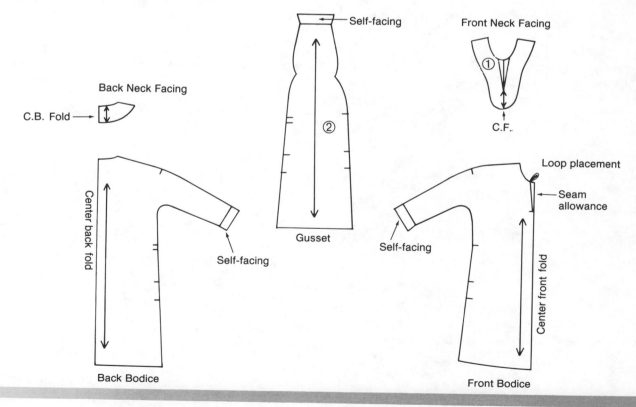

Five

The "Big Shirt"

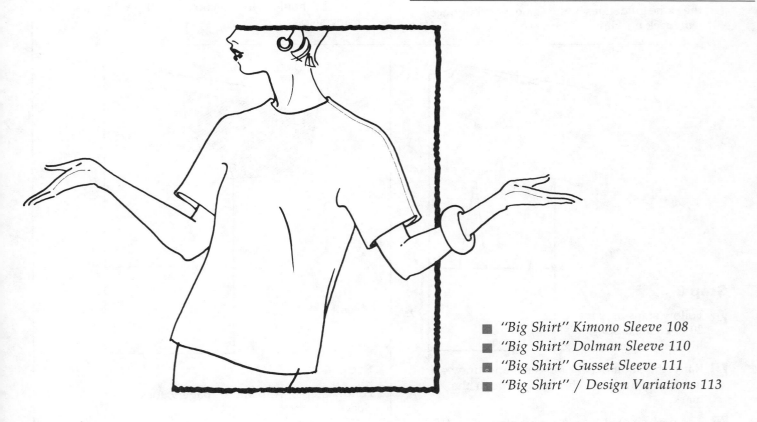

"**B**ig Shirt" Kimono Sleeve

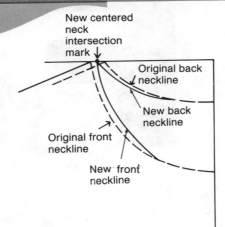

Step 1

The two-dart front bodice is used as basis for creating perfectly balanced front and back kimono patterns which have the looser "big shirt" look found styles. The front shoulder dart is pivoted into the armhole and used as ease, which contributes to overall looser fit.

A Pivot shoulder dart of two-dart front bodice into lower third of the armhole.

B On paper draw a horizontal and a vertical guideline at a right angle.

C Place center front against vertical guideline, with its neck/shoulder intersection touching horizontal guideline. Trace front bodice.

D Place back bodice over front, matching it to the same guidelines in the same way, but trace *only* back neckline.

Step 2

A If the front and back neck/shoulder intersections touch each other, go on to Step 3.

B If they do not touch, mark the center of their difference, and blend new front and back necklines from that centered mark into the original necklines. That mark will serve as the neck/shoulder intersection for all the following steps.

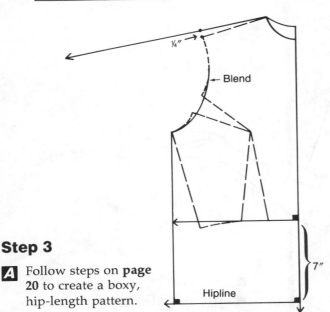

Step 3

A Follow steps on **page 20** to create a boxy, hip-length pattern.

B Raise the shoulder ¼" for ease, and draw an indefinite line from the neck through the ¼" mark.

C The dart pivoted into the armhole will be left in as ease. Blend a new armhole across the open dart.

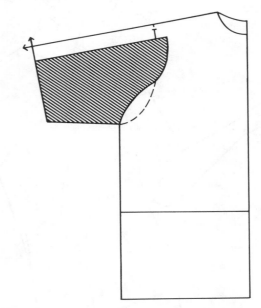

Step 4

Follow Step 6, A, B and C, **page 9,** for the sleeve.

. . . The Smarter They Fall

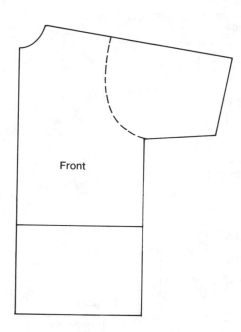

Front

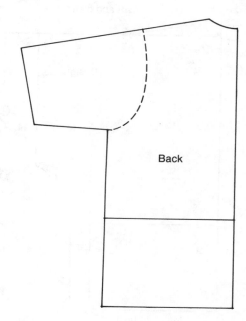

Back

Step 5

A Trace the front pattern. Flip the front bodice over, and mark that side as the right side.

B Trace the back pattern, using all the seams of the front bodice except for back neckline. The side seams will now face each other, a positioning that makes for easier use of the bodices when designing.

The "big shirt" pattern can be used for many designs where kimono looseness is desired. The fact that the front and back are perfectly balanced allows for easier patternmaking of even the most complex designs.

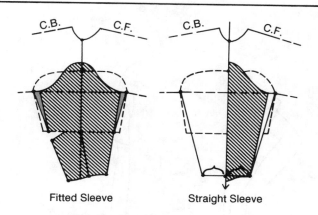

Fitted Sleeve

Straight Sleeve

All adjustments made to the fitted kimono bodice can be applied to the "big shirt" also. See **pages 14** and **15**.

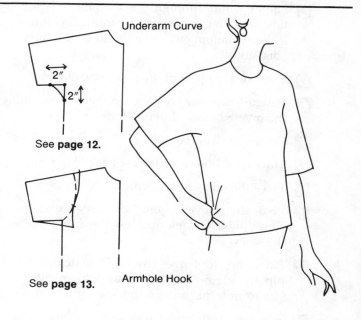

Underarm Curve

2"

2"

See **page 12.**

See **page 13.**

Armhole Hook

"**B**ig Shirt" Dolman Sleeve

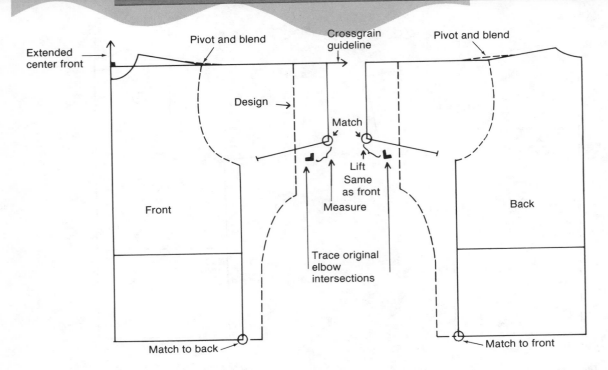

To create a dolman sleeve on a "big shirt," follow all the steps for the dolman sleeve, **pages 44** and **45** (the steps are reviewed briefly below).

A Trace only bodice section of front "big shirt."

B Trace the elbow intersection.

C Square a line through the shoulder intersection from an extended center front. Crossgrain is the minimum guideline for lift on a dolman "big shirt."

D Pivot sleeve up until it lies on squared line.

E Measure the distance between the original and the pivoted elbow intersections.

F Design the desired dolman silhouette.

G Trace only bodice section of back "big shirt."

H Trace the elbow intersection.

I Pivot the sleeve up until the distance at the elbow intersections matches the front. Trace the sleeve.

J Place the front over the back, matching the hip and elbow corners. Trace dolman silhouette from front through to back.

K Separate front and back, and continue with any other design features desired.

Note: The batwing variation can be created on the "big shirt" by following the steps for The Batwing Sleeve & Fitted Bodice, **page 66,** and The Batwing Sleeve & Hip-Length Pattern, **page 67.**

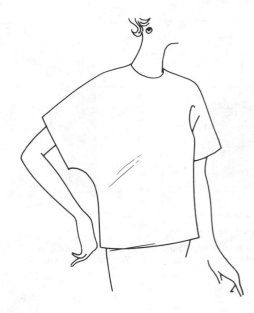

"Big Shirt" Gusset Sleeve

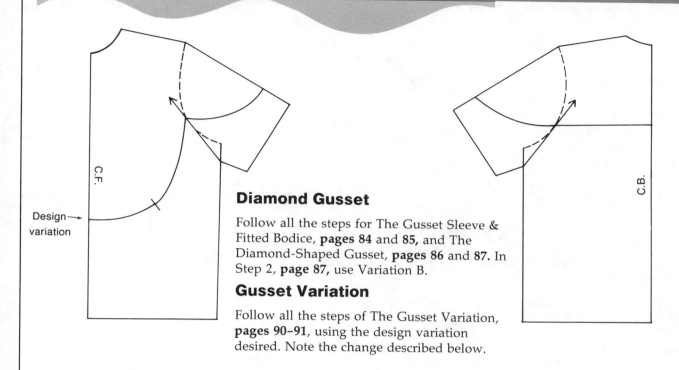

C.F.

Design variation

C.B.

Diamond Gusset

Follow all the steps for The Gusset Sleeve & Fitted Bodice, **pages 84** and **85,** and The Diamond-Shaped Gusset, **pages 86** and **87.** In Step 2, **page 87,** use Variation B.

Gusset Variation

Follow all the steps of The Gusset Variation, **pages 90–91,** using the design variation desired. Note the change described below.

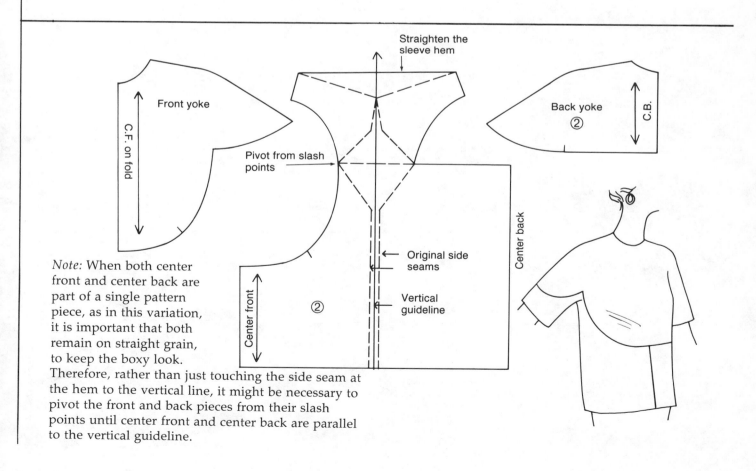

Straighten the sleeve hem

Front yoke

C.F. on fold

Pivot from slash points

Back yoke ②

C.B.

Center back

Original side seams

Vertical guideline

Center front ②

Note: When both center front and center back are part of a single pattern piece, as in this variation, it is important that both remain on straight grain, to keep the boxy look. Therefore, rather than just touching the side seam at the hem to the vertical line, it might be necessary to pivot the front and back pieces from their slash points until center front and center back are parallel to the vertical guideline.

Design Variations

"Big Shirt" Kimono Sleeve

DESIGN VARIATION

Design Features

- "Big shirt" kimono overblouse with arm-hole seams
- Roll-up sleeves
- Side seams are extended into ties at hem

Basic Patterns

- Trace the "big shirt" patterns, **pages 108** and **109**, shoulder seam to shoulder seam, and draw in armhole seamlines as illustrated below. See **page 12** for armhole seams.

Draft

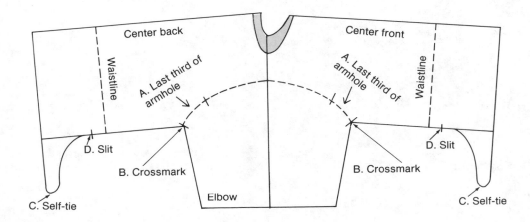

Step 1

A Divide front and back armhole into equal thirds and crossmark the last third on front and back.

B Crossmark the front and back underarm intersections.

C Design ties as desired.

D Mark crossmarks for slit openings on the side seam.

Step 2. Underarm Ease

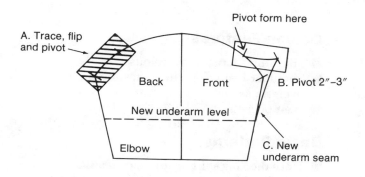

Trace the sleeve section of the "big shirt" created in Step 1.

A Trace the lower third of the back armhole on a separate piece of paper, and flip the paper over. (The tracing is demonstrated here on the back, and the flipping and pivoting are demonstrated on the front.)

B Pivot up the traced armhole 2"–3" between the underarm crossmarks. Repeat A and B for the front.

C Draw a new underarm seam to touch the original underarm at the desired level.

Step 3. Roll-up Cuff

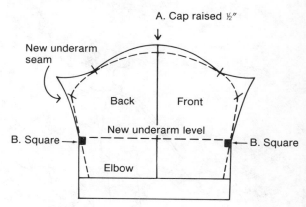

A Raise the cap ½" and connect it to the lower third front and back cap.

B Square down from the new underarm level to the desired length of the sleeve. (Roll-up sleeves should be rectangular.)

Patterns

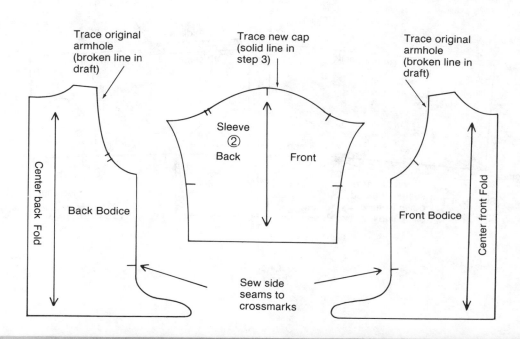

DESIGN VARIATION

"Big Shirt" Kimono Sleeve

Design Features

■ "Big shirt" kimono overblouse
■ Shoulder band that eliminates the original overarm seams
■ Welt pockets

Basic Patterns

■ Trace the "big shirt" pattern, **pages 108** and **109,** shoulder seam to shoulder seam, and draw seamlines as illustrated below.

Draft

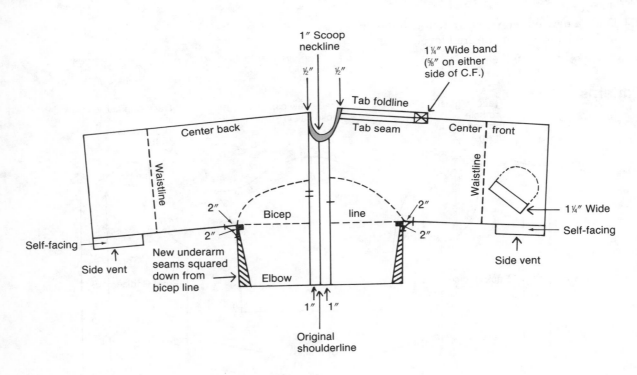

Patterns

Shoulder Band

Back
②

Center back

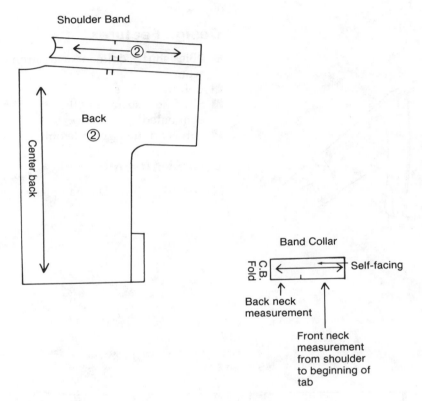

Band Collar

C.B.
Fold

Self-facing

Back neck
measurement

Front neck
measurement
from shoulder
to beginning of
tab

Right Tab

Left Tab

①

①

C.F.

C.F.

Self-facing

Front
②

C.F.

Welt

②

Self-facing

Pocket

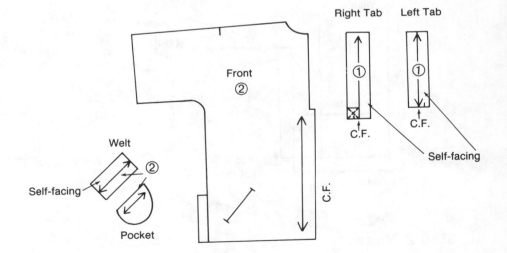

"Big Shirt" Dolman Sleeve

Design Features

- "Big shirt" dolman with front princess seam
- Roll-up sleeves
- Shoulder seam of the yoke has been eliminated
- Tab is on the right side only

Basic Patterns

- The "Big Shirt" Dolman Sleeve, **page 110**

**Drafts
Step 1**

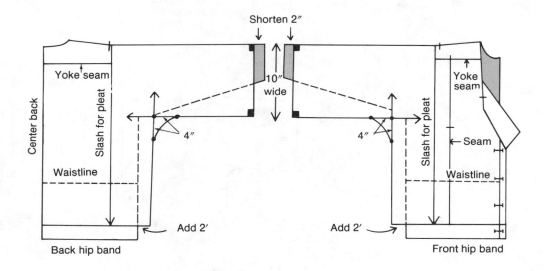

Step 2. Yoke

A Trace the front yoke section.

B Join the front yoke to the back yoke, shoulder to shoulder, and trace the entire yoke as one piece.

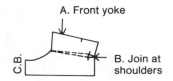

A. Front yoke

C.B.

B. Join at shoulders

Step 3

Cut away the yoke section. Slash on the pleat line to the hem. Spread the amount desired.

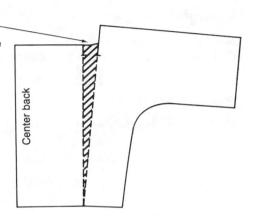

Cut away the yoke section. Slash on the pleat line to the hem. Spread the amount desired.

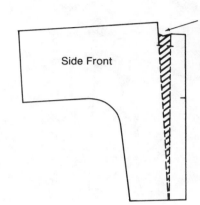

Patterns

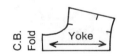

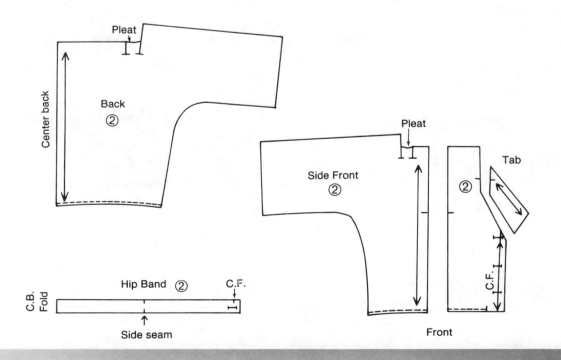

"Big Shirt" Dolman Sleeve

Design Features

■ "Big shirt" dolman
■ Long sleeves with cuffs that button on the overarm seam

Basic Patterns

■ The "Big Shirt" Dolman Sleeve, **page 110**

Drafts

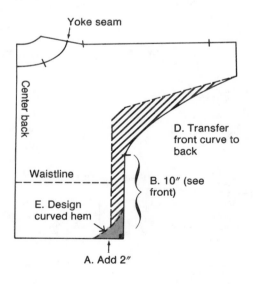

Yoke seam

Center back

D. Transfer front curve to back

Waistline

B. 10" (see front)

E. Design curved hem

A. Add 2"

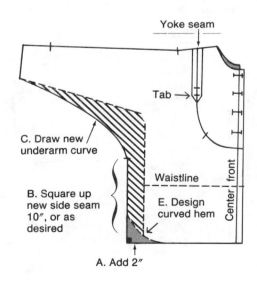

Yoke seam

Tab →

C. Draw new underarm curve

B. Square up new side seam 10", or as desired

Waistline

Center front

E. Design curved hem

A. Add 2"

Patterns

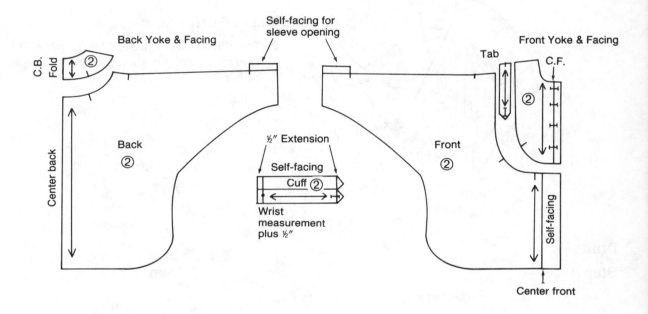

"Big Shirt" Dolman Sleeve

DESIGN VARIATION

Design Features

■ "Big shirt" with a stylized gusset that becomes a button tab

Basic Patterns

■ The "Big Shirt" Gusset Sleeve, **page 111,** except design the seamlines as illustrated below

Drafts

Step 1

Step 2 . Gusset

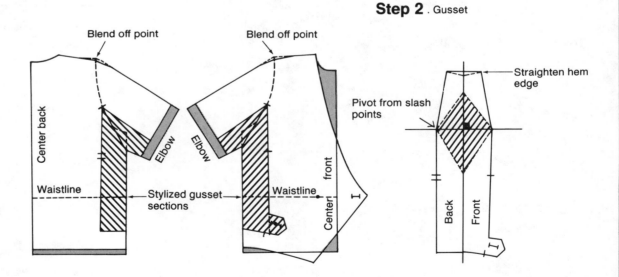

Patterns

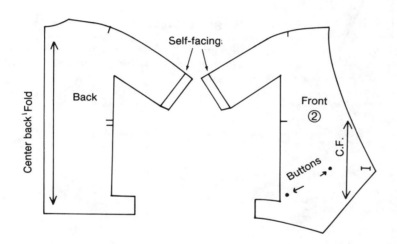

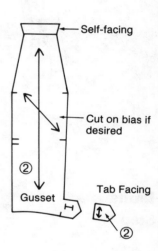

"Big Shirt" House Gusset

Design Features

- ■ "Big shirt" with a gusset that forms a loose jacket
- ■ Inverted pleat at center back
- ■ Front vents allow front panels to be tucked in or left loose
- ■ Back yoke and sleeve cut in one-piece

Basic Patterns

- ■ The "Big Shirt" Gusset Sleeve, **page 111**, except design the seamlines as illustrated below

Drafts
Step 1

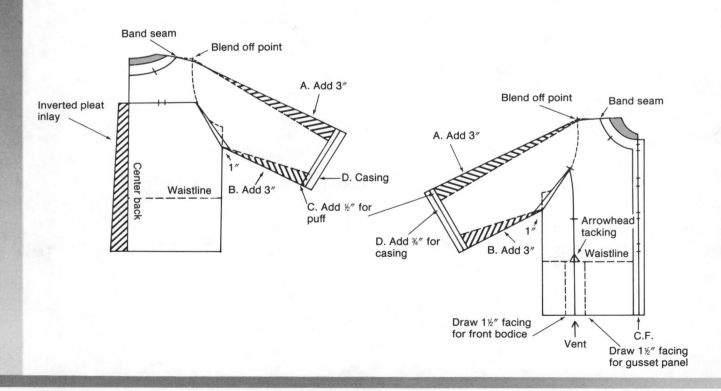

Step 2

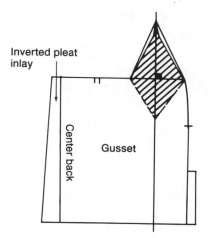

Trace front and back gusset sections, and cut them out. Follow instructions **page 111.**

Step 3

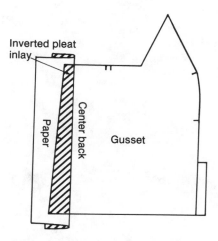

Develop inset by placing center back on folded paper, and tracing the inverted pleat inlay. Unfold. (See pattern below.)

Patterns

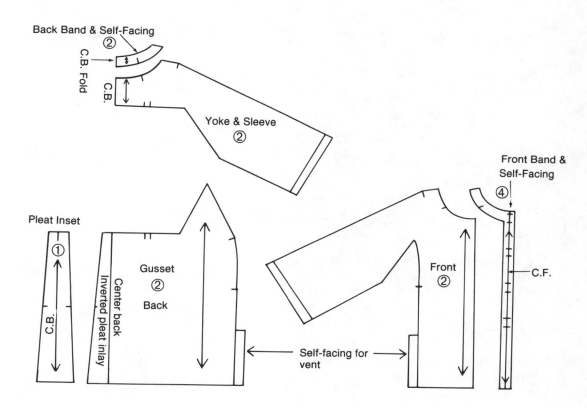

DESIGN VARIATION

S_{ix}

The Semi–
Set–In Sleeve

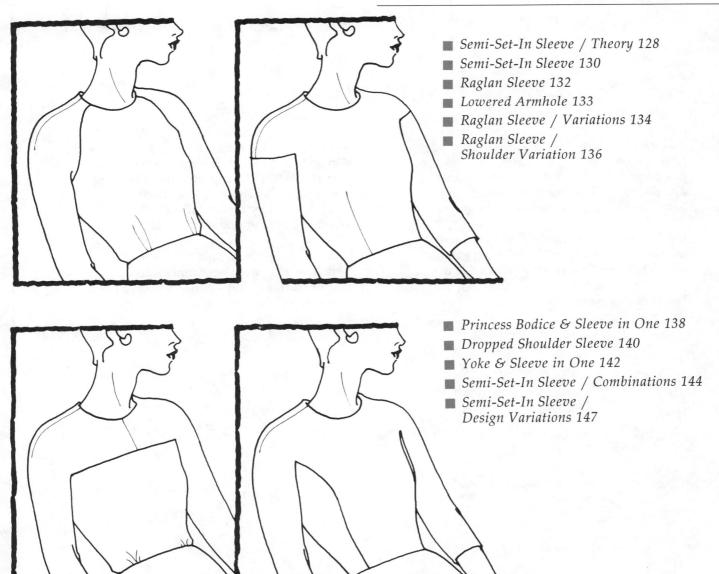

Semi-Set-In Sleeve/Theory

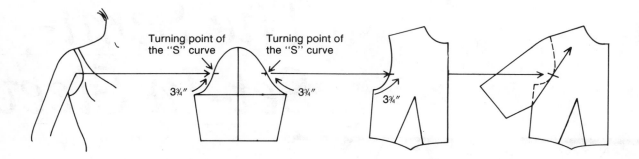

The muscle which joins the arm to the body is the pivoting point of the arm, and it is a key point to locate on sleeves and bodices. The diagrams show the muscle point on the *body*, the *sleeve*, the *bodice*, and the *gusset*.

On the sleeve, the muscle points are located at the turning points of the "S" curves which form the cap. These turning points define where the underarm section of the cap becomes the overarm section, or, in other words, where the muscle is. The muscle can also be found by a short-cut method: measure 3¾" up the cap from the bicep line, front and back. On the bodice, the muscle point is found by measuring 3¾" up the armhole from the side seam, front and back.

The 3¾" short-cut method of locating the muscle is very useful, but it helps to know that the turning point of the "S" curve of the sleeve cap is the actual muscle point.

On a gusset bodice (diagram 1), a slash is made up *to* the muscle point, which allows for inserting the diamond-shaped gusset, and restoring the lift to the sleeve.

If, on the same gusset bodice (diagram 2), a slash were made up *from* the muscle point (to the neck, for example), and the underarm and side seam lengths were restored, the bodice and sleeve pieces could be separated. The resulting patterns, with a seam to the neck, would be the raglan sleeve. If the seam had been drawn to the overarm, the separated pattern would be the dropped shoulder sleeve. A seam toward the center front would create the yoke and sleeve in one piece, and a seam to the dart apex would create the princess bodice and sleeve in one piece.

A set-in sleeve has a more downward silhouette, since its overarm can be lengthened when the seam is drawn to the tip of the shoulder. The other sleeves illustrated do not have their overarm seam lengthened, since they do not go to the tip of the shoulder. They, therefore, retain a more outward silhouette, which is a distinguishing feature of all semi-set-in sleeves.

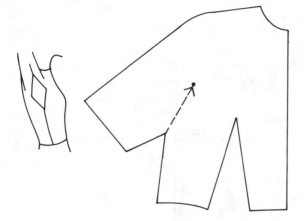

1. Sleeve lowered with slash up *to* the muscle.

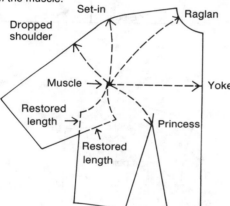

2. Sleeve lowered with seams up *from* the muscle.

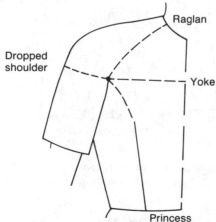

3. Bodice showing several semi-set-in sleeve design variations.

Note: On the actual semi-set-in sleeve draft, the silhouette will be even more downward than on a gusset bodice, which was used here just for illustration

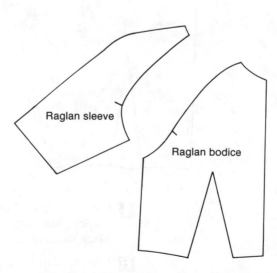

Example of a semi-set-in sleeve (the raglan) taken from diagram 2.

Semi-Set-In Sleeve

The theory of the semi-set-in sleeve discussed on the preceding pages explains its development from a gusset bodice, but it is better in actual practice to develop the sleeve from separate bodices and a sleeve, as shown here. This method produces the same result, but allows for more control in each step of the process. The silhouette created by this method is similar to that of a gusset bodice with its sleeve pivoted further downward, a silhouette which falls between that of the gusset sleeve and that of the set-in sleeve (see **page 3**).

For All Semi-Set-In Sleeves:

A Trace a fitted sleeve, elbow length if desired, and extend its center line up a short distance.

B Measure up 3¾″ on the front and back cap, from the bicep line intersection. Mark the muscle points.

Step 1

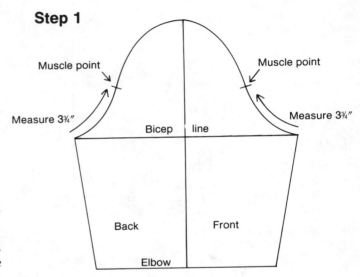

Step 2

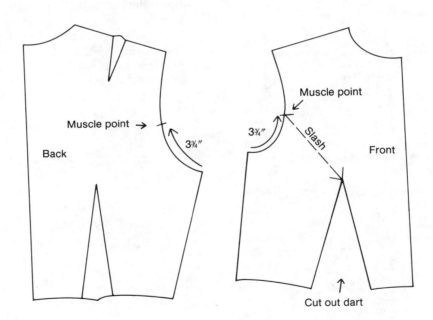

A Using the back bodice and the one-dart front bodice, measure up 3¾″ on each armhole. Mark the muscle points.

B Cut out dart pickup from front waist dart.

C Slash a line from the front muscle point to the dart apex.

Touch and Go

Step 3

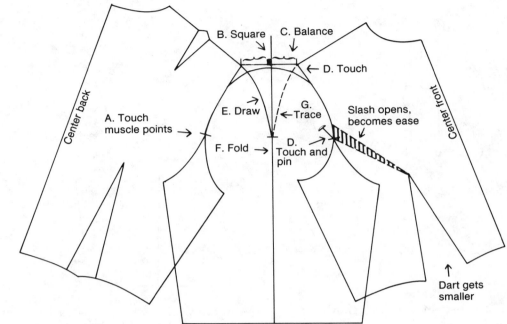

The Basic Semi-Set-In Sleeve

A Touch the back bodice muscle point to the back sleeve muscle point, and place the upper armhole against the upper cap. (*Do not* overlap the bodice and sleeve, as that would tighten the garment. Just place them together so that they meet.) Trace the back bodice.

B Square a line from the extended sleeve center line to the back shoulder corner. Measure that distance.

C Repeat that distance on the other side of the sleeve center line. Place a mark at that balanced point.

D Touch and pin the front bodice muscle point to the front sleeve muscle point. Then touch the front shoulder corner to the balanced mark on the squared line drawn in C. (See enlarged diagram.) The slashed line will open to allow these two points to meet, and the cut-out waist dart will automatically get smaller. The space created by the opened slash remains in the armhole as ease. Trace the front bodice.

E Use a french curve to draw a shoulder seam from the end of the back shoulder to the sleeve's center line at the muscle point level.

F Fold the front bodice and sleeve under on the sleeve center line.

G Trace the back shoulder curve onto the front. Because the shoulders have been balanced,

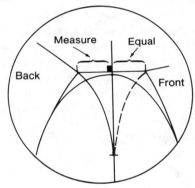

the traced curve will touch the front shoulder corner. The semi-set-in sleeve is now ready for designing, which begins on the next page. The basic semi-set-in sleeve *must* be changed into a design since it cannot be separated until a seam is drawn.

Note:

1 The space between the shoulder curves is the ease of the cap, which is discarded in semi-set-in sleeves.

2 The semi-set-in sleeve can also be developed using any hip-length pattern. The shoulder dart on the hip-length pattern is cut out rather than the waist dart, and it is the shoulder dart that gets smaller as the slash from the muscle point opens.

Raglan Sleeve

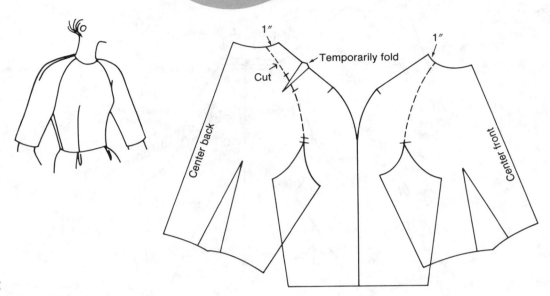

The Draft

A Develop the semi-set-in sleeve as shown on **pages 130** and **131**.

B The necessary lines of that sleeve are shown here as solid lines. The other lines used for developing the sleeve, such as the upper armholes and sleeve cap, have been left out of this diagram. (The upper sleeve cap will be replaced by the raglan seam in this example.)

C Design basic raglan seams as desired from the muscle point to the neck (*Ill:* 1″ from the shoulder), front and back. On the back, tem-

porarily fold and close the back shoulder dart before designing the raglan curve. The curve will be cut from the neck through the folded dart, and the dart will remain permanently closed in the raglan sleeve's shoulder section. Any dart remaining in the bodice can be eased in during construction.

D Crossmark the muscle points, doubling them on the back to identify the back piece.

E Trace the bodice and sleeve sections separately to create the patterns.

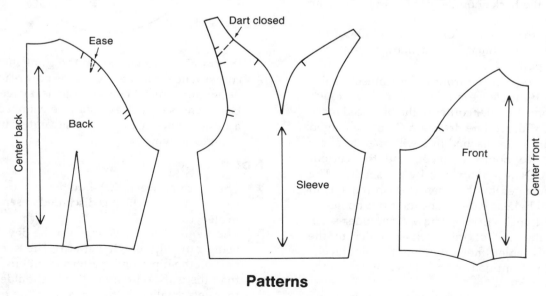

Patterns

Lowered Armhole

1

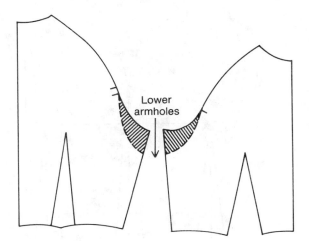

For the lowered armhole sleeve, which can be created on any set-in or semi-set-in sleeve, first lower the armholes on the bodice at the side seams, front and back, the desired distance. (*Suggested maximum: 3″.*) Redraw the armholes from the muscle points to the lowered side seams.

2

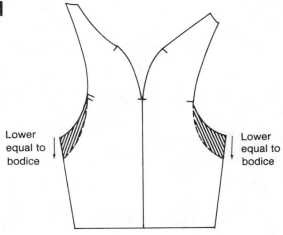

Lower the same desired distance on the underarm seams of the sleeves. Redraw the armholes from the muscle points to the lowered underarm seams.

3

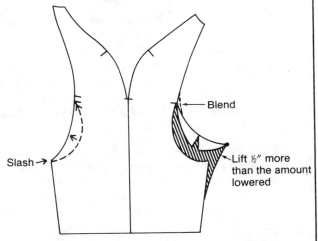

The lowered sleeve cap now matches the lowered bodice armholes in length, but the shortened underarm seams of the sleeve will restrict its lift. The length of the underarm seams must be restored. To restore the underarm seam lengths, and return the lift to the sleeve, follow the instructions for Underarm Ease **page 135,** except lift each bicep corner ½″ more than the amount the underarm seams were lowered in Step 1, to guarantee that sufficient lift is restored.

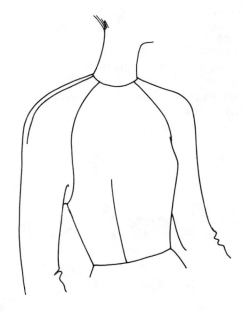

Raglan Sleeve Variations

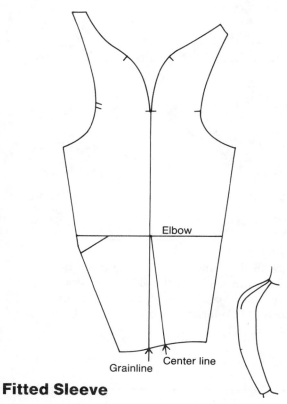

Fitted Sleeve

The elbow-darted fitted sleeve can be used when setting up the semi-set-in sleeve.

If an elbow-length sleeve is used, as it is in this text, it can be changed into a full-length sleeve simply by placing a fitted sleeve pattern over the elbow-length sleeve, matching the elbow lines, and tracing the fitted sleeve from the elbow to the wrist.

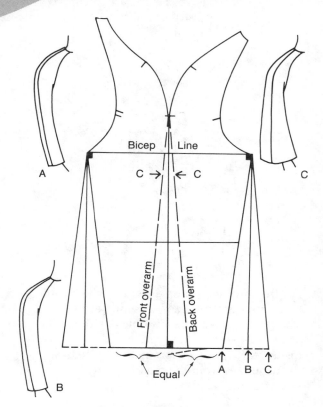

Straight & Flared Sleeves

A This straight sleeve is the narrowest sleeve that can be made without an elbow dart. Trace just the front of the full-length fitted sleeve. Square a line from the grainline to the front wrist corner. Measure the squared line, and repeat that measurement on the other side of the grainline. Connect this new wristline to the back bicep intersection.

B The narrow straight sleeve just created can be changed into a perfectly squared sleeve by squaring down two new underarm seams from the bicep line, and then widening the wristline to meet the new underarm seams.

C The sleeve may be widened slightly further by adding balanced flare to the squared sleeve at both the underarm and overarm seams. Add equal amounts to the squared underarm seams, and draw new underarm seams to the bicep line. Add equal amounts of flare to the overarm seam at the wrist, and then draw new front and back overarm seams by connecting those flares to the shoulder. (Pivot a ruler from the flares until the ruler touches the shoulder.)

. . . and Short of It

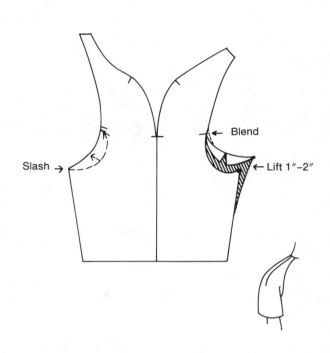

Underarm Ease

For a more casual look and a looser fit, ease can be added to the underarm of any semi-set-in sleeve design.

The underarm seam is lengthened, and the bicep is widened, to loosen the fit of the sleeve, and to create more lift for the arm. Draw semi-circular slash lines from the bicep corners to the front and back muscle points. The curves can be 1½" deep at their widest points. Then draw another, straight, slash line from the widest part of each curve across to each armhole.

Cut each curved slash line, and each straight slash line. Lift each bicep corner equally, the amount desired, usually 1" to 2". (The diagram shows the lift on the front only, but it must be done on the back also.) The straight slash line will open to allow the armhole to remain curved.

Draw new, balanced underarm seams from the lifted bicep corners down to the elbow level. Blend the muscle points.

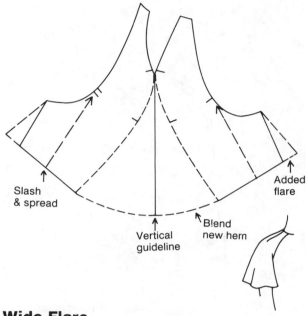

Wide Flare

The raglan's shoulder seams form a dart, which, like any other dart, can be pivoted to a new location.

The shoulder seam dart can be transferred to the hem of the sleeve to create a wide flared sleeve. This method works best with a short sleeve since a very wide amount of flare is introduced. The longer the sleeve, the wider that flare would be.

Create a short raglan sleeve, and split it along its center line into separate front and back sleeves.

Place the front and back sleeves on either side of a vertical guideline. Starting at the endpoint of the shoulder seam dart, pivot that dart closed by touching the curved front and back shoulder seams to each other.

Stop pivoting when the desired amount of flare has been transferred into the hem, balanced on either side of the vertical guideline. Additional flare can be distributed into the hem by slashing and spreading up to the muscle points, and by adding flare to the underarm seams. Blend the new flared hemline.

Raglan Sleeve/Shoulder Variation

Getting the Bold Shoulder

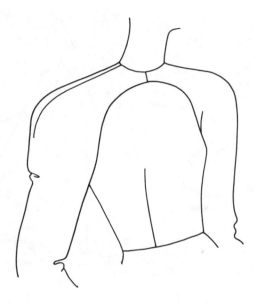

The overarm seam of the raglan sleeve can be varied endlessly, as may the shape of the raglan seam itself. Two variations are illustrated here.

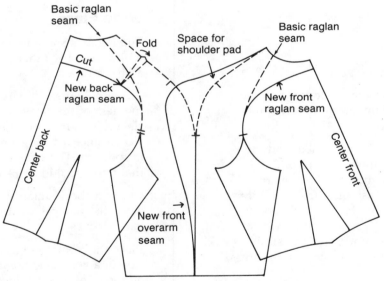

Step 1

Design new front and back raglan seams as desired. (The broken lines in the diagram represent the basic raglan seams created in **Step C, page 132.**) The best raglan designs are smooth, continuous curves that begin at the muscle points. (The back shoulder dart can be hidden in a back raglan seam if that seam touches the dart's apex.)

Step 2

Design a new front shoulder seam as desired. It can be raised for a shoulder pad, then rounded or pointed as it tapers down toward the hem of the sleeve.

Step 3

Extend the sleeve center line upward. Fold the front under on that line, and trace the new front overarm seam. Unfold. True in the traced overarm seam, which then becomes the back overarm seam. Since the front and the back neck intersections are not balanced and cannot be matched on the fold, trace the front overarm seam from the extended center line to the neck, on another piece of paper. Flip the traced paper over, matching the center line/shoulder intersections, and pivot it until the front neck/shoulder intersection touches the back shoulder seam. Trace the front shoulder seam onto the back bodice.

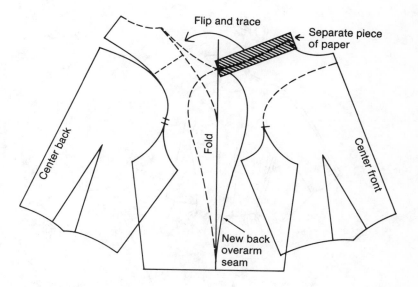

Patterns

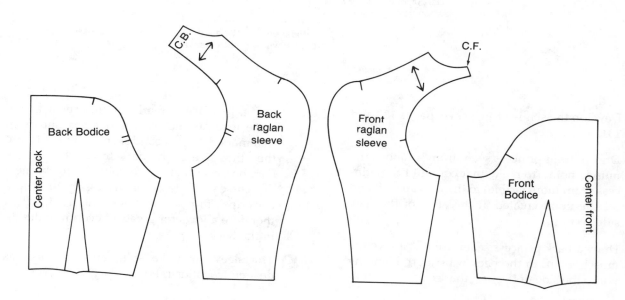

Princess Bodice & Sleeve in One

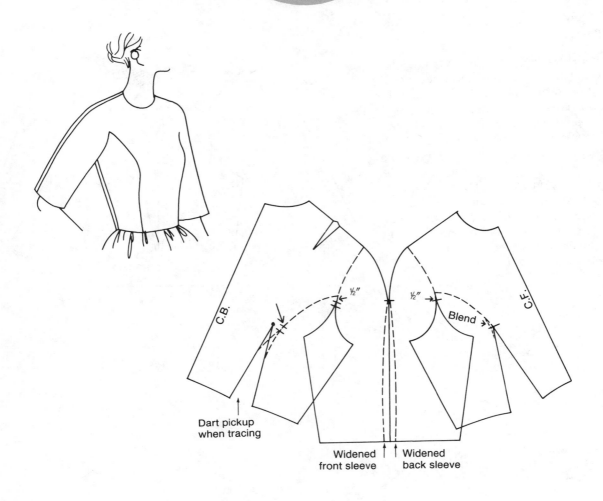

C.B.

Dart pickup
when tracing

½"   ½"

Blend

C.F.

Widened
front sleeve   Widened
back sleeve

1 Develop the semi-set-in sleeve, **pages 130** and **131.**

2 Draw a front princess seam from ½" above the muscle point (to make that corner of the princess seam more visible) to the dart apex. Blend off the point created at the apex of the new side section.

3 Draw a back princess seam from ½" above the muscle point to the back waist dart, blending it into the side of the dart that is closest to cen-ter back. Place a mark on this seam at the same level as the back dart apex, and from that mark draw a second seam that blends into the other side of the dart. In effect, the back dart has been curved to conform to the new design seam. It is not as necessary to keep a back apex in place as it is in the front, which therefore allows for greater freedom of design in the back.

4 The sleeve may be split, and widened, as desired (see illustration).

Patterns (without seam allowances)

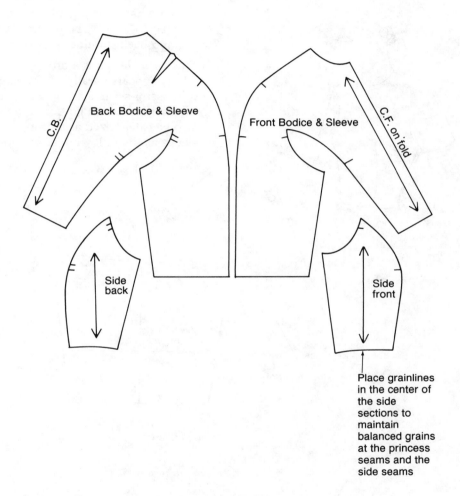

C.B.

Back Bodice & Sleeve

Front Bodice & Sleeve

C.F. on fold

Side
back

Side
front

Place grainlines
in the center of
the side
sections to
maintain
balanced grains
at the princess
seams and the
side seams

Dropped Shoulder Sleeve

Basic Design

1 Develop the semi-set-in sleeve, **pages 130** and **131**.

2 From ½″ above the front and back muscle points (to ensure the visibility of the design corners) draw a gently curved seam that connects those ½″ points to the end of the front and back shoulder seams (see dots).

This basic design is a dropped shoulder seam which appears parallel to the floor. Any other semi-set-in sleeve variation in which the designed seam goes into the sleeve can also be categorized as a dropped shoulder sleeve as the following page illustrates.

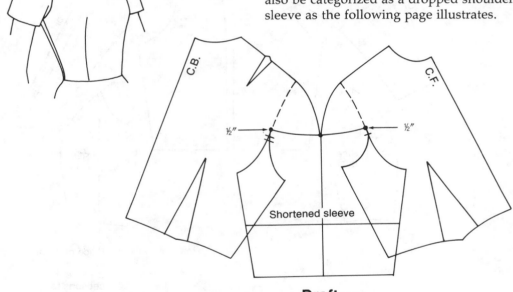

Draft

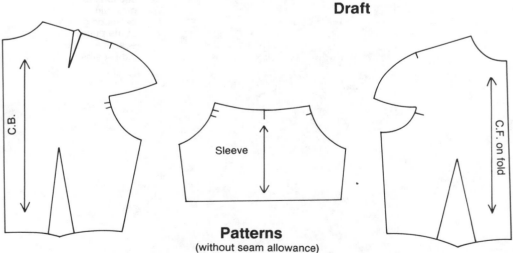

Patterns
(without seam allowance)

Variations

The dropped shoulder seam can be designed in a great variety of ways, starting from the muscle point or any other point along the cap up to near the shoulder seam, and ending anywhere on the sleeve from just off the shoulder to the wrist.

Once the dropped shoulder section is created, the remaining sleeve section can be shortened, or slashed and spread for puff or flare, or eliminated completely for a sleeveless dropped shoulder design.

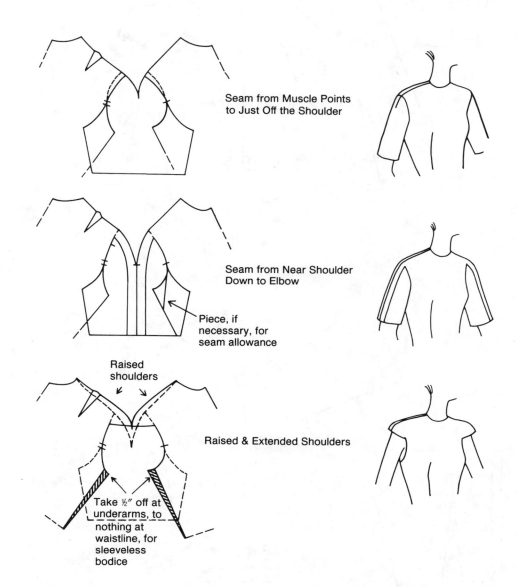

Seam from Muscle Points to Just Off the Shoulder

Seam from Near Shoulder Down to Elbow

Piece, if necessary, for seam allowance

Raised shoulders

Raised & Extended Shoulders

Take ½" off at underarms, to nothing at waistline, for sleeveless bodice

Yoke & Sleeve in One

Basic Design

1 Develop the semi-set-in sleeve, **pages 130** and **131.**

2 Draw yoke seams by squaring lines from center back and center front that touch the armholes ½" above the muscle points (to ensure the visibility of the design corners).

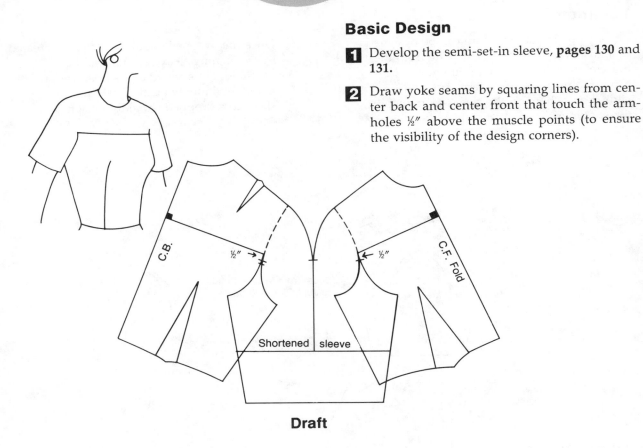

Draft

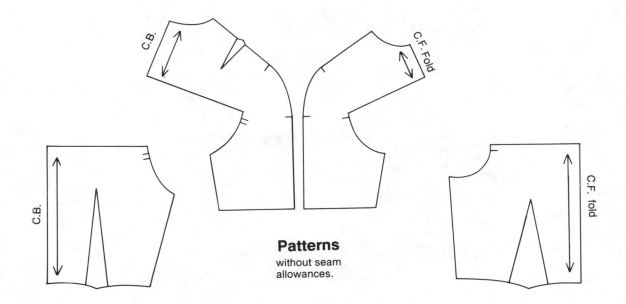

Patterns
without seam
allowances.

of Fancy

Variations

The squared yoke is a classic design for the yoke and sleeve in one piece, but any designed seam that goes toward the center front and center back, squared or not, places that design into this category of sleeve.

A yoke and sleeve seam can start anywhere from the muscle point, or any other point along the cap up to near the shoulder seam, and continue to the center front and the center back anywhere from the neckline to the waistline.

The sleeve can be made any length, and the shoulder seam styled as desired.

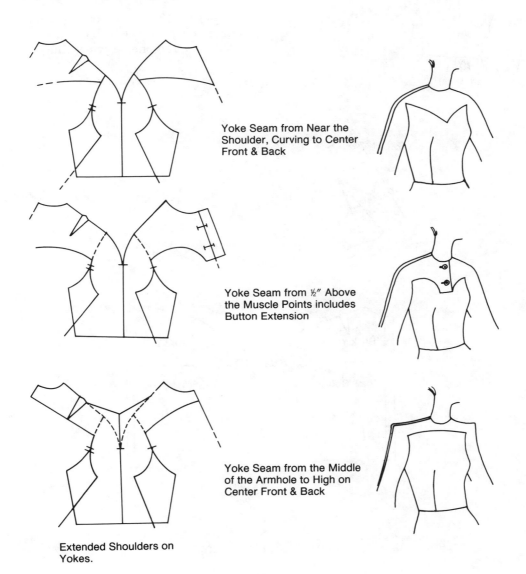

Yoke Seam from Near the Shoulder, Curving to Center Front & Back

Yoke Seam from ½" Above the Muscle Points includes Button Extension

Yoke Seam from the Middle of the Armhole to High on Center Front & Back

Extended Shoulders on Yokes.

Semi-Set-In Sleeve/Combinations

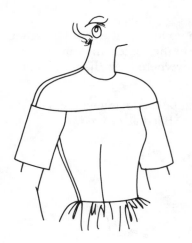

Dropped Shoulder & Yoke

The dropped shoulder sleeve, and the sleeve and yoke in one piece can be combined into one design. A dropped shoulder seam and yoke seam can be drawn through the semi-set-in sleeve.

See **pages 140** and **142** for instructions on the individual sleeves, which can then be combined into one design as illustrated.

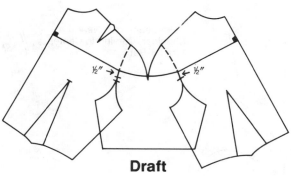

½" →   ← ½"

Draft

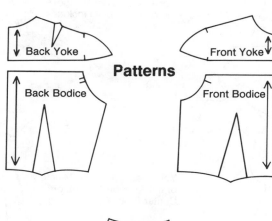

Back Yoke

Front Yoke

Patterns

Back Bodice

Front Bodice

Sleeve

Dropped Shoulder & Princess Bodice

To combine the dropped shoulder sleeve with the princess bodice and sleeve in one, see **pages 138** and **142** for the individual instructions, and then follow the diagrams on this page as a guide for the new design. Any variation of the dropped shoulder sleeve or princess bodice and sleeve can be used, in addition to the basic design illustrated here.

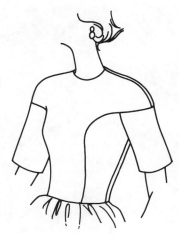

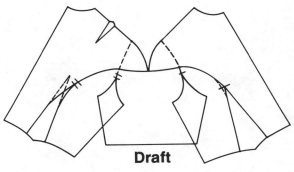

Draft

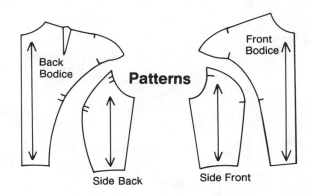

Back Bodice

Front Bodice

Patterns

Side Back

Side Front

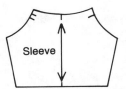

Sleeve

Design
Variations

Raglan Sleeve

DESIGN VARIATION

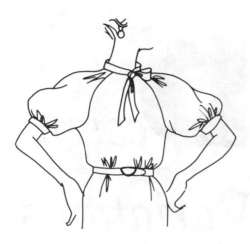

Design Features

■ Gathers at the shoulders of the push-up raglan sleeves are held by a neck band tied in a bow at center front

Basic Patterns

■ The Raglan Sleeve, **page 132**
■ The puffed sleeve with Underarm Ease and Wide Flare, developed from **pages 134** and **135**

Draft

Step 1

Redraw dart on raglan seam. Fold new dart closed. True back neckline. Unfold.

Crossmark opening for neck tie bow

Center back

Center front

Elbow

Step 2

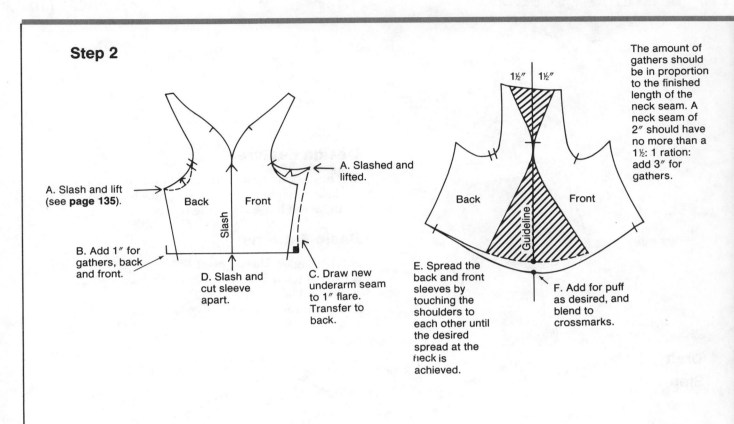

A. Slash and lift (see **page 135**).

Back   Front

Slash

B. Add 1″ for gathers, back and front.

D. Slash and cut sleeve apart.

C. Draw new underarm seam to 1″ flare. Transfer to back.

A. Slashed and lifted.

1½″   1½″

Back   Front

Guideline

E. Spread the back and front sleeves by touching the shoulders to each other until the desired spread at the neck is achieved.

F. Add for puff as desired, and blend to crossmarks.

The amount of gathers should be in proportion to the finished length of the neck seam. A neck seam of 2″ should have no more than a 1½: 1 ration: add 3″ for gathers.

DESIGN VARIATION

Patterns

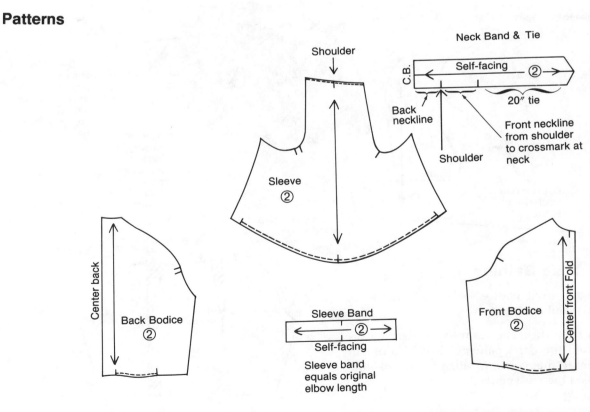

Shoulder

Sleeve ②

Center back

Back Bodice ②

Neck Band & Tie

C.B.

Self-facing ②

Back neckline

Shoulder

20″ tie

Front neckline from shoulder to crossmark at neck

Sleeve Band

②

Self-facing

Sleeve band equals original elbow length

Front Bodice ②

Center front Fold

Raglan Sleeve

DESIGN VARIATION

Design Features

■ The asymmetrical front bodice of this design makes it necessary to trace both the right and left sides of the bodice.

Basic Patterns

■ The Raglan Sleeve, **page 132**
■ The Raglan Sleeve / Shoulder Variation, **pages 136** and **137**
■ Underarm Ease, **135**

Draft
Step 1

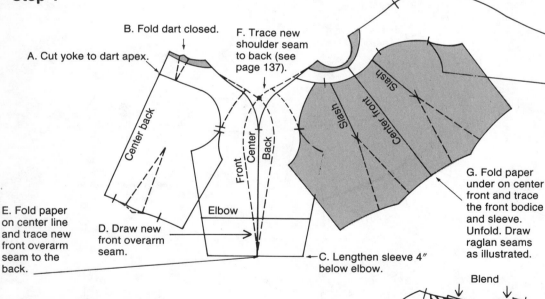

B. Fold dart closed.

A. Cut yoke to dart apex.

F. Trace new shoulder seam to back (see page 137).

Center back

E. Fold paper on center line and trace new front overarm seam to the back.

D. Draw new front overarm seam.

Front · Center · Back

Elbow

C. Lengthen sleeve 4″ below elbow.

Slash

Center front

Slash

H. Draw slash lines from raglan seams to the dart apexes. Indicate crossmarks for gathers

G. Fold paper under on center front and trace the front bodice and sleeve. Unfold. Draw raglan seams as illustrated.

Step 2. Yoke Gathers

A Trace the front bodice section (shaded area, Step 1), and cut it out.

B Slash from the yoke seam to the dart apexes and fold the darts halfway closed, to obtain gather at the yokeline. Blend the yokeline between the crossmarks.

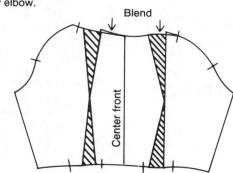

Blend

Center front

Step 3 Underarm Ease (optional)

Right Front Sleeve

← B. Blend

A. Slash & lift 1"–2"

C. Repeat on left front sleeve & back sleeve

For more freedom of movement, the sleeve underarm seams may be lengthened. See page 135 for complete instructions.

Patterns

C.B.

Back Sleeve & Yoke

Choice of grainlines (parallel to C.B. or along overarm seam)

Center back

Back Bodice ②

Right Front Sleeve

① Choice of grainlines

Front Bodice ①

Center front

C.F.

① Choice of grainlines

Left Front Sleeve

Raglan Sleeve with Lowered Armhole

DESIGN VARIATION

Design Features

- Raglan sleeve with lowered armholes

Basic Patterns

- The Raglan Sleeve, **page 132**
- The Lowered Armhole, **page 133**

Draft Step 1

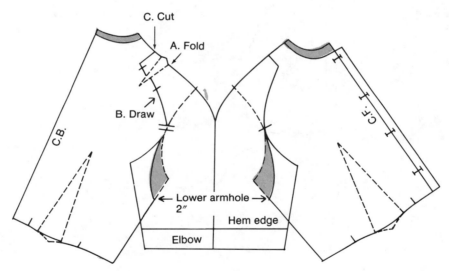

A Fold the back shoulder dart closed.

B Draw a raglan seamline over the folded dart.

C Cut the raglan seamline to the dart. The dart remains folded in the sleeve. The remainder of the dart on the back bodice becomes ease.

D See Step 1, **page 133.**

Step 2. Lowered armhole
See Step 2, **page 133**

Step 3. Underarm ease
See Step 3, **page 135**

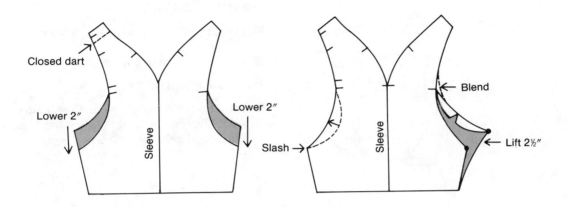

Patterns

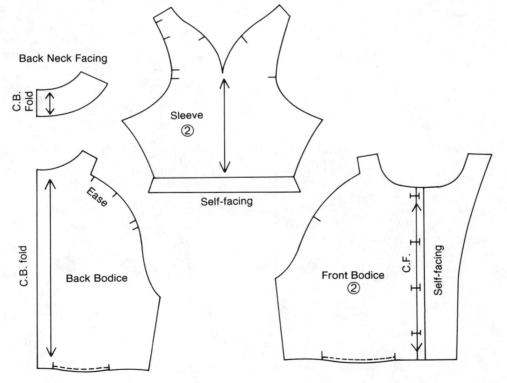

Princess Bodice & Sleeve in One

Design Features

■ Front princess seams designed toward center front

■ Bodice with an asymmetrical closing

Basic Patterns

■ Princess Bodice & Sleeve in One, **pages 138** and **139,** except design the seamlines as illustrated below.

Draft

A. Blend dart into princess line, see Step 3, **page 138.**

B. Design neckline and lapel. Fold paper under on the neckline and trace the lapel. The left front bodice will be traced along the neckline only.

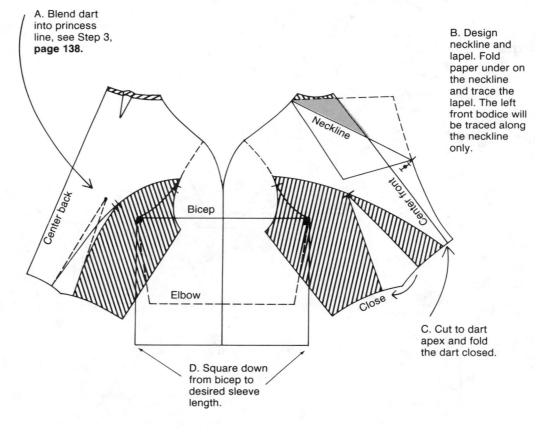

Center back

Neckline

Center front

Bicep

Elbow

Close

C. Cut to dart apex and fold the dart closed.

D. Square down from bicep to desired sleeve length.

Patterns

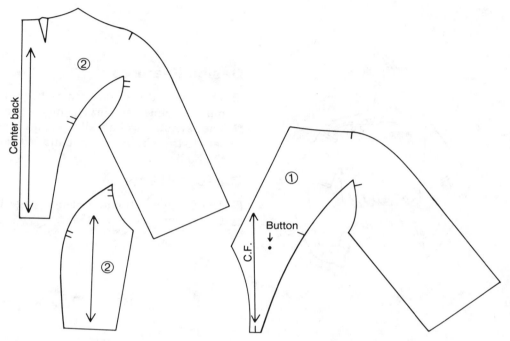

Back Bodice & Side Back

Left Front Bodice

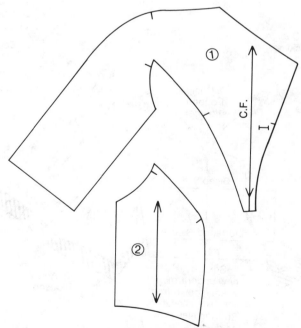

Right Front Bodice & Side Front

Dropped Shoulder Sleeve

Design Features

■ The dropped shoulder seams begin at the muscle points and curve gently upward.
■ The asymmetrical neckline makes it necessary to trace both the right and left sides of the bodice.

Basic Patterns

■ The Dropped Shoulder Sleeve, **page 140**
■ Underarm Ease, **page 135**

Draft

Step 1

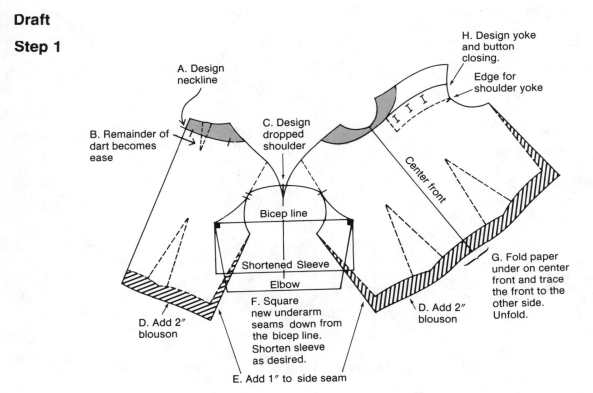

A. Design neckline

H. Design yoke and button closing.

Edge for shoulder yoke

B. Remainder of dart becomes ease

C. Design dropped shoulder

Center front

Bicep line

G. Fold paper under on center front and trace the front to the other side. Unfold.

Shortened Sleeve

Elbow

F. Square new underarm seams down from the bicep line. Shorten sleeve as desired.

D. Add 2″ blouson

D. Add 2″ blouson

E. Add 1″ to side seam

Step 2 Underarm ease (optional)

For more freedom of movement, the sleeve underarm seam may be lengthened. See **page 131** for complete instructions.

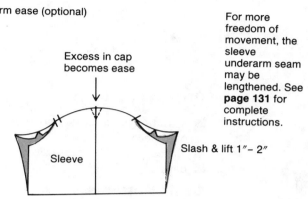

Excess in cap becomes ease

Sleeve

Slash & lift 1″– 2″

Patterns

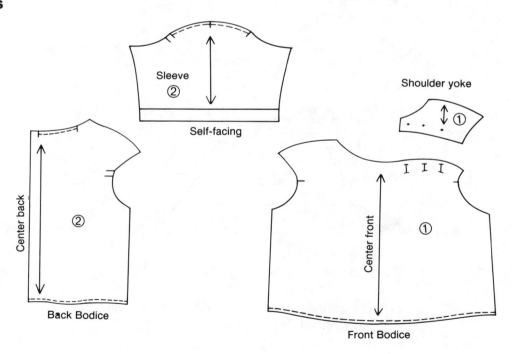

Sleeve ②

Self-facing

Shoulder yoke ①

Center back

Back Bodice ②

Center front

Front Bodice ①

Yoke & Sleeve in One

Design Features

- Variation of a classic yoke and sleeve-in-one piece
- Flared sleeves
- Lapped neckline

Basic Patterns

- The Yoke & Sleeve in One, **page 142**

Draft Step 1

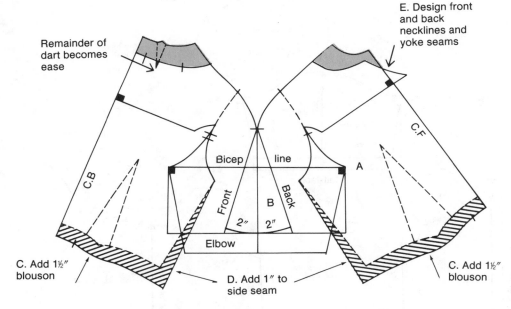

Remainder of dart becomes ease

E. Design front and back necklines and yoke seams

Remainder of dart becomes ease

Bicep line

C.B

C.F

Front

Back

B

A

2″ 2″

Elbow

C. Add 1½″ blouson

C. Add 1½″ blouson

D. Add 1″ to side seam

A Square down new underarm seams from the bicep line.

B Add 2″ flare to the front and back overarm seams. Blend sleeve hems.

Patterns

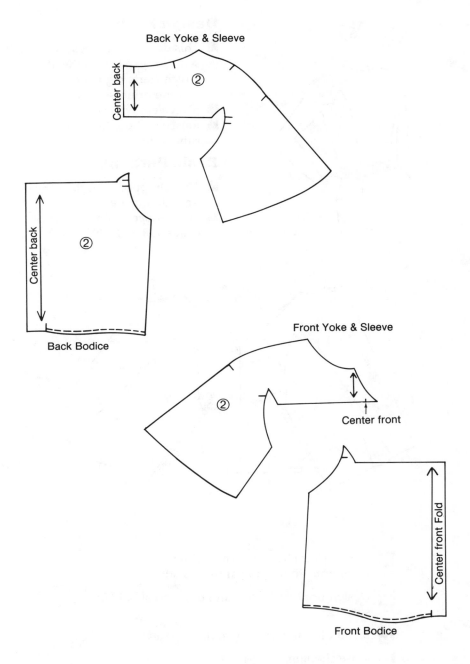

Back Yoke & Sleeve

Center back

②

Center back

②

Back Bodice

Front Yoke & Sleeve

②

Center front

Center front Fold

Front Bodice

Semi-Set-In Sleeve Combination

DESIGN VARIATION

Design Features

■ This design combines two variations of the semi-set-in sleeve: the dropped shoulder which starts high above the muscle points, and the princess seam.
■ Sleeveless bodice
■ Raised shoulder for an exaggerated silhouette

Basic Patterns

■ The Dropped Shoulder Sleeve / Design Variation, **page 141**
■ The Princess Bodice & Sleeve in One, **pages 138** and **139**

**Draft
Step 1**

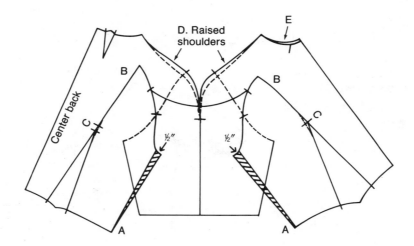

A For a sleeveless bodice, tighten ½" at the underarms to nothing at the waistline.

B Design princess bodice and dropped shoulder seams.

C Blend off point at original dart apexes.

D Raise shoulder as desired.

E Indicate crossmark for beginning of band collar.

Step 2. Band Collar

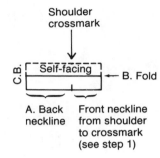

Shoulder crossmark

C.B. Self-facing ← B. Fold

A. Back neckline

Front neckline from shoulder to crossmark (see step 1)

A Draw a rectangle the length required and the height desired. (*Ill: 1″.*)

B Fold paper back on collar edge and trace the collar for a self-facing.

DESIGN VARIATION

Patterns

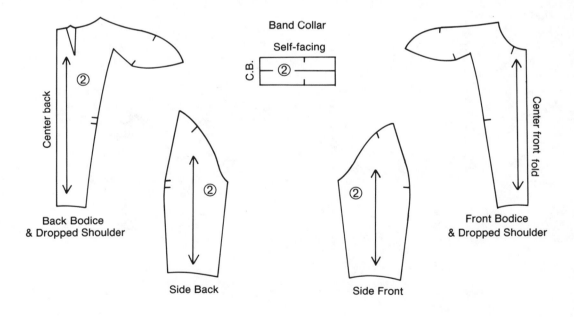

Center back

②

Back Bodice & Dropped Shoulder

Side Back

②

Band Collar

Self-facing

C.B. ②

②

Side Front

Center front fold

②

Front Bodice & Dropped Shoulder

Collar–in–
One with
the Bodice

S*even*

The Shawl Collar

Collar-in-One with the Bodice/Theory

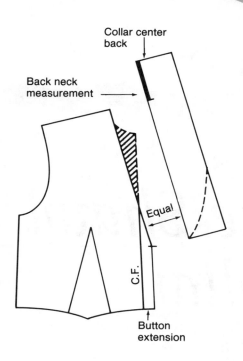

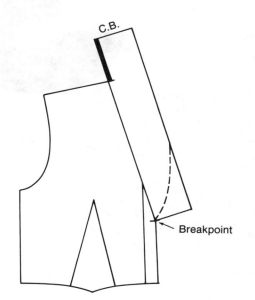

The collar-in-one with the bodice, known as the shawl collar, can be thought of, in theory, as a separate rectangular collar placed against the "V" neckline of the bodice, and then cut together as one piece.

Step 1

If a bodice with a button extension has a "V" neckline drawn on it, the measurement of that neckline can be used to create a rectangle of equal length, which would then be extended by the length of the back neckline. The collar's center back measurement (explained on **page 168**), would be used to create the two shorter sides of the rectangle. The end of the rectangle, closer to the button extension, could be shaped as desired (see broken line curve in the rectangle).

Step 2

The rectangle could then be placed against the "V" neckline of the bodice, and the whole shape cut as one piece.

The point where the "V" neckline meets the beginning of the collar is called the *breakpoint*.

. . . and One for Shawl

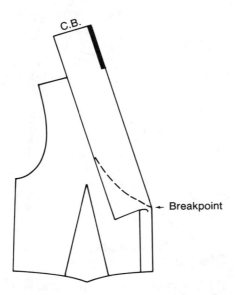

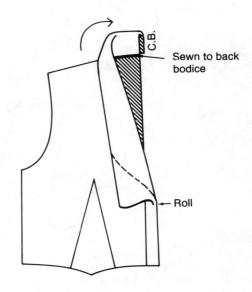

Step 3

To create the finished look of the shawl collar in fabric, the rectangle would first be folded over onto the bodice on the "V" neckline, from the breakpoint to the neck/shoulder intersection.

Step 4

The advantage of the one-piece collar and bodice is that when the collar is folded over (Step 3) and then turned at the shoulder to be sewn to the back bodice neckline, a tension develops along the "V" neckline which causes the collar to roll attractively at the breakpoint. If the rectangle were sewn to the bodice instead, the neckline seam would cause the breakpoint to lay flat.

The separate sewn shawl collar is most often used on blouses and dresses, while the shawl collar-in-one with the bodice is most often found on suit and coats, where the heavier-weight fabrics hold the roll well.

The following pages describe the actual steps needed to create the shawl collar.

Stand Shawl Collar

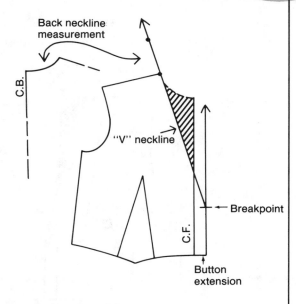

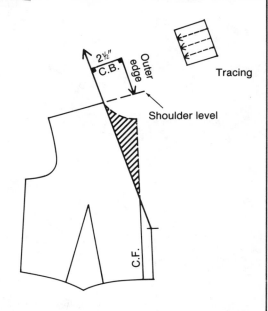

There are three basic types of collars: the *stand,* which lies against the neck; the *flat,* which lies against the shoulder; and the *roll,* which combines both, lying against the neck and then rolling over to touch the shoulder. Each type will be discussed individually. (A complete discussion on separate collars can be found in our companion text, *Basic Pattern Skills for Fashion Design.*)

The stand collar is basically a rectangle, because that is the shape that represents, on paper, the cylindrical form of the neck.

Step 1

A Trace the front bodice desired.

B Draw a button extension. *Rule:* for horizontal buttonholes, the extension equals the diameter of the button.

C Mark the breakpoint where desired on the button extension.

D Draw a "V" neckline from the breakpoint to the neck/shoulder intersection, extending it indefinitely beyond that point.

E Measure the back bodice neckline, and mark that measurement on the indefinite line, starting at the neck/shoulder intersection.

Step 2

A The center back of the collar is always squared from the back neckline, to ensure a smooth, continuous neckline when the collar is completed. Square an indefinite line for the collar center back from the end of the back neck measurement just marked.

B On a collar designed to lie against the neck, as in this example, the stand is usually 1"—anything higher than that can be uncomfortable. A perfectly rectangular collar will fold exactly in half, so that a 1" stand will have a 1" fall, or foldover. That means, however, that the folded collar will not cover the neck seam. Therefore, the collar should not be a perfect rectangle, but one whose outer edge is at least ¼" longer than the neck edge. The collar will now fold over less than half, and cover the neck seam by about ½". A 1" stand will then have a 1½" fall, and a total center back measurement of 2½". To prepare a non-rectangular collar, mark off 2½" on the squared center back line.

C Square a line down from the 2½" point to the shoulder level of the bodice. Make a tracing of the back collar from center back to the shoulder level, and divide that tracing into equal fourths. Slash each fourth from the outer edge to the neckline.

. . . Divided We Shawl

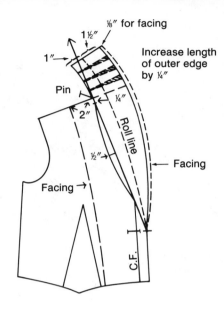

Step 3

A Pin the tracing to the bodice at the neck/shoulder intersection, and spread the outer edge until it is at least ¼" longer than the back neckline. Trace around the spread section.

B Place a mark on center back equal to the height of the stand (*Ill:* 1"). Continue marking off that measurement, parallel to the neckline, as far as the shoulder level, to indicate the roll line on which the collar will fold over. From the shoulder level, continue the roll line to nothing at the breakpoint.

C The in-one cut of the collar causes a "bubble" of fabric to form along the "V" neckline. A "fish dart" must be created to flatten the fabric. Measure ¼" down the "V" neckline from the neck/shoulder intersection (to avoid sewing into that corner). Find the center between that ¼" mark and the point where the "V" neckline crosses center front, and from that center point measure off ½" in toward the bodice. Connect the ¼" to the ½" to the center front crossing point with a smooth curve (the dart is curved on its bodice side, and straight on its neckline side).

D The facing, which is the top collar, is made ⅛" larger around the outer edge than the under collar to hide the seam at that edge.* Taper to nothing at the breakpoint. Mark off 2" from the neck/shoulder intersection, and draw curved line to the waistline, for the inner facing edge.

Patterns (without seam allowances)

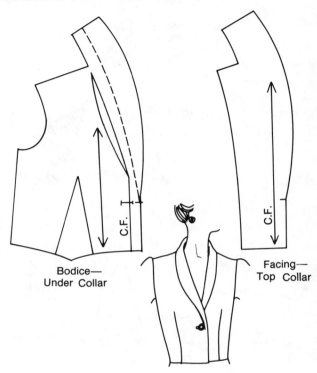

Bodice—
Under Collar

Facing—
Top Collar

E Design the collar from the shoulder level to the breakpoint. Mark the buttonholes, placing the first one at the breakpoint level to ensure that the collar will be held there.

Step 4

On finished bodice mark: roll line (important if tailoring is required along the stand), "fish dart," buttonhole markings, straight grain, center front, breakpoint crossmark.

On facing mark: breakpoint crossmark, grainline, and center front. The facing becomes the top collar on shawl designs.

The "fish dart" is marked only on the bodice, which is the undercollar, as it would show if it were sewn on the top collar. Similarly, the roll line is used as a guide on the undercollar only. Buttonhole markings are not necessary on the facing since they are cut through from their bodice placement.

*Add ⅛" for medium-weight fabrics—more for heavier-weights.

Roll Shawl Collar

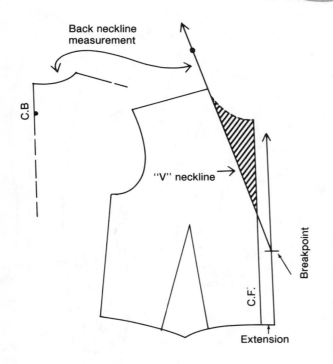

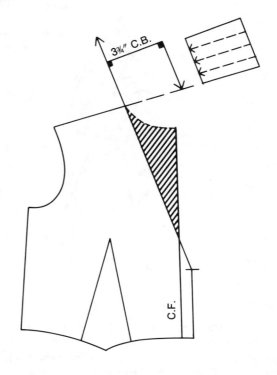

Step 1

A A roll shawl collar is cut with its center back on bias for a soft roll onto the shoulder. A bias center back means that the outer edge is longer than the neck edge, changing the original rectangular shape so that the collar folds in thirds rather than in half. In other words, a bias collar will stand for one-third of its center back length, and fall for two-thirds of that length. For example, a 3″ long collar will stand for 1″ and fall for 2″.

B Follow Step 1, A, B, C, D and E, **page 168.**

Step 2

A Follow Step 2, A, **page 168.**

B The center back of a collar designed directly against the neck can be 3″–4″, rather than the 2½″ of the stand shawl collar, since the bias collar folds in thirds rather than in half. (*Ill:* 3¾″ C.B. Once folded, the stand is 1¼″, and the fall 2½″.)

C Square a line down from the end of the center back to the shoulder level.

D Trace the back collar, divide the tracing into fourths, and slash each fourth.

... We'll Shawl You

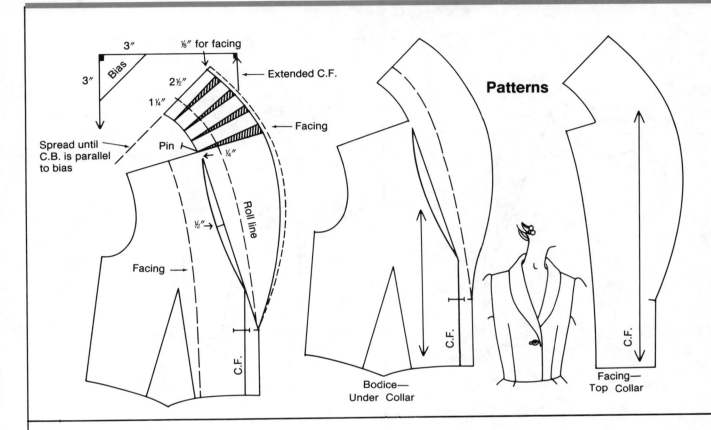

3″
⅛″ for facing
Bias
3″
2½″
Extended C.F.
1¼″
Patterns
Facing
Spread until
C.B. is parallel
to bias
Pin
¼″
Roll line
½″
Facing
C.F.
C.F.
C.F.
Bodice—
Under Collar
Facing—
Top Collar

Step 3

A To establish a bias guideline, extend center front straight up indefinitely (straight grain). At a point high above the bodice, square across an indefinite line (cross grain). At a point beyond the bodice, square down a short line (straight grain).

B From the intersection just created, measure an equal amount in each direction (*Ill:* 3″ by 3″). Draw a line connecting these equal measurements for a bias guideline.

C Pin the traced back collar to the neck/shoulder intersection, and spread the outer edge until the collar's center back is parallel to the bias guideline.

D Trace around the spread sections, then unpin and remove.

E Place a mark up from the center back/neckline intersection equal to one-third of center back (*Ill:* 1¼″), and continue marking off that measurement from center back to the shoulder level, always parallel to the neckline, to indicate the roll line. From the shoulder level, continue the roll line to nothing at the breakpoint.

F To complete the draft and pattern, follow Step 3, C, D and E, and Step 4, **page 169.**

Flat Shawl Collar

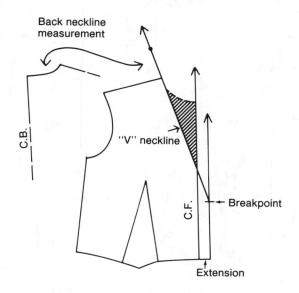

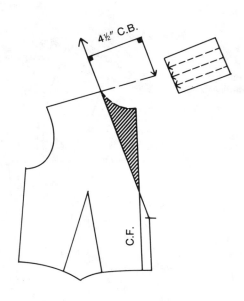

Step 1

A A flat shawl collar is cut with its center back on straight grain to ensure enough width on its outer edge for the collar to lay flat against the bodice.

B Follow Step 1, A, B, C, D and E, **page 168.**

Step 2

A Follow Step 2, A, **page 168.**

B The center back on a flat collar can be any length desired, since the collar will not have a stand. (*Ill:* 4½″ C.B.)

C Square down from the end of center back to the shoulder level.

D Trace the back collar, divide the tracing into fourths, and slash each fourth.

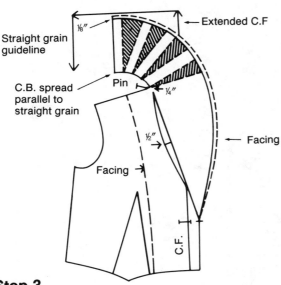

Straight grain guideline

⅛″

← Extended C.F

C.B. spread parallel to straight grain

Pin

¼″

½″

← Facing

Facing →

C.F.

Step 3

A To establish a straight grain guideline, follow Step 3, A, **page 171.**

B Pin the tracing to the bodice at the neck/ shoulder intersection, and spread the outer edge until the collar's center back is parallel to the straight grain guideline.

C Trace around the spread sections, then unpin and remove.

D To complete the draft and pattern, follow Step 3, C, D and E, and Step 4, **page 169.**

Note: There is no roll line on a flat collar.

CENTER BACK FOR SHAWL COLLARS

	C.B. Grain	C.B. Stand	C.B. Length
STAND	off grain; spread outer edge ¼″ wider	1″ (against the neck)	2½″
ROLL	spread to bias	one-third of the C.B. length	three times the stand
FLAT	spread to straight grain	0	any length

Patterns

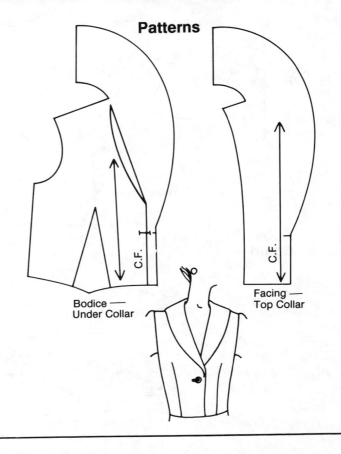

C.F.

Bodice — Under Collar

C.F.

Facing — Top Collar

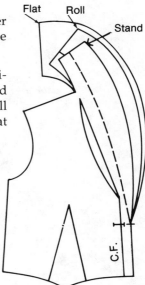

The three collars—*stand, roll* and *flat*—when superimposed as shown here, demonstrate two principles:

1 The longer the outer edge, the flatter the collar.

2 Stand collars are basically rectangles, and fold nearly in half; roll collars fold in thirds; flat collars have no stand.

Note: On roll collars, the stand is one-third of the collar's center back. Therefore, the longer the center back is, the higher the stand will be.

Flat Roll

Stand

C.F.

Shawl Collar with Standaway Neckline

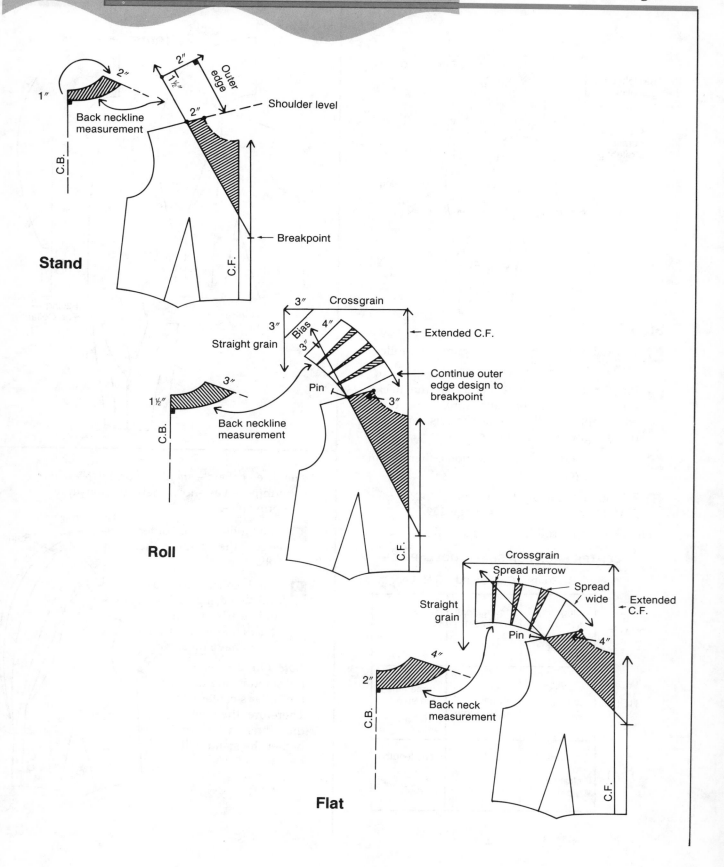

Stand

Roll

Flat

. . . Off Your Chest

Stand

A Widen the front neckline as desired (*Ill: 2"*).

B Widen the back neckline an equal amount at the shoulder.

C Lower center back one-half the amount lowered at the shoulder, to create a bateau neckline. This neckline allows the collar to frame the face.

D Design a new back neckline, squaring it off for a short distance at the center back, and then curving it into the shoulder. Measure the new neckline.

E Follow Step 1, **page 168,** substituting the new back neckline measurement when marking off on the extended "V" neckline.

F The collar's center back length can vary as desired, since its stand will not be uncomfortable on this standaway neckline. (*C.B. Length Ill: 3½".*)

G Follow the remaining steps, **pages 168** and **169,** to complete the collar.

Note: On standaway collars the outer edge will always be longer than the neck edge, due to the angle of the "V" neckline which tilts the rectangle toward bias and lengthens the outer edge. Therefore, the tracing, slashing and spreading of the rectangle will not be necessary; the stand will always be less than half of center back.

Stand

Roll

A Follow Steps A, B, C, D and E of the stand collar above. The standaway neckline illustrated is 3".

B The collar's center back length can vary as desired (*Ill: 6"*), keeping in mind that the stand will be one-third of that length.

C Follow Steps 2 and 3 of the roll collar, **pages 170** and **171,** to complete the draft and pattern. The stand on the collar illustrated here is 2", which is one-third of the 6" used in this design.

Note: On some variations, depending on the angle of the "V" neckline, the center back of the collar rectangle will be on bias, and no slashing and spreading will be necessary.

Roll

Flat

A Follow Steps A, B, C, D and E of the stand collar above. The standaway neckline illustrated is 4".

B The collar's center back can vary as desired, since the collar will not have a stand.

C Follow Steps 2 and 3 of the flat collar, **pages 168** and **169,** to complete the draft and pattern.

Note: When the back neckline is bateau-shaped, it is best to spread the slashed tracing into a similar bateau shape. To accomplish this, give the most spread to the slash near the shoulder, which will curve that section, and the least spread to the slashes near the collar's center back, which will somewhat straighten that section and thus create a collar neckline similar in shape to the back bodice neckline.

Flat

Design
Variations

Roll Shawl Collar with Standaway Neckline

Design Features

- Roll shawl collar with a standaway neckline on a yoke
- Dolman sleeves

Basic Patterns

- The Shawl Collar with Standaway Neckline, **pages 174** and **175**
- The Dolman Sleeve, **pages 44** and **45**

Drafts

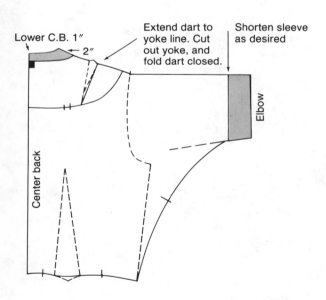

Lower C.B. 1″

Extend dart to yoke line. Cut out yoke, and fold dart closed.

Shorten sleeve as desired

2″

Elbow

Center back

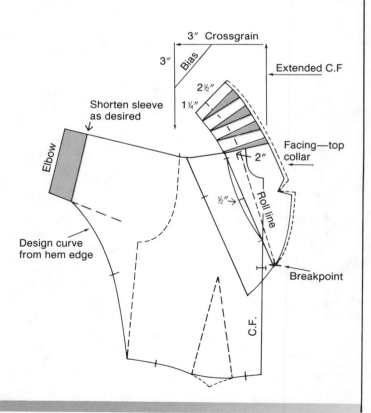

3″ Crossgrain

3″ Bias

Extended C.F

2½″

1¼″

Facing—top collar

Shorten sleeve as desired

Elbow

2″

½″

Roll line

Design curve from hem edge

Breakpoint

C.F.

Patterns

Back Yoke & Bodice

Back yoke is self-faced

C.B. Fold

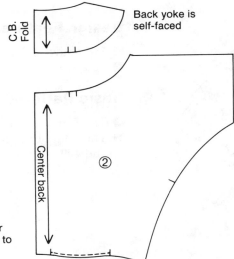

Center back

②

Back zipper inserted up to yoke seam

Yoke & Under Collar

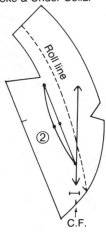

Roll line

②

C.F.

Facing—Top Collar

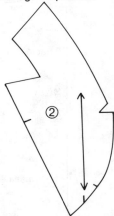

②

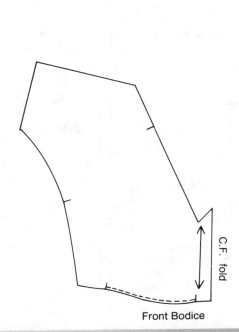

C.F. fold

Front Bodice

Flat Shawl Collar

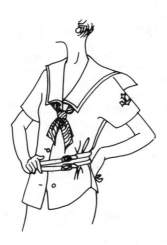

Design Features

- ■ Flat shawl sailor collar
- ■ "Big shirt" overblouse

Basic Patterns

- ■ The Flat Shawl collar, **pages 172** and **173**
- ■ The "Big Shirt" Kimono Sleeve, **pages 108** and **109**

Drafts

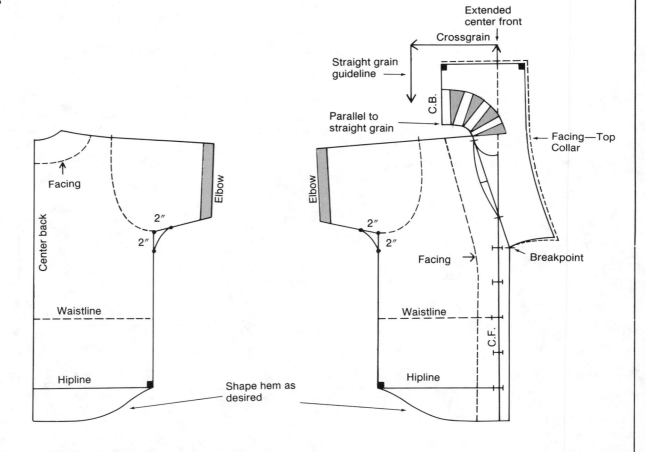

Patterns

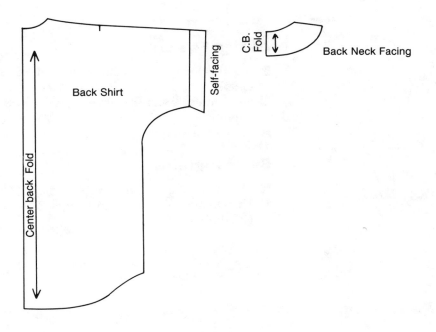

Back Shirt

Center back Fold

Self-facing

C.B. Fold

Back Neck Facing

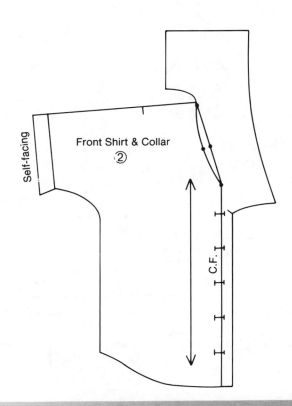

Self-facing

Front Shirt & Collar
②

C.F.

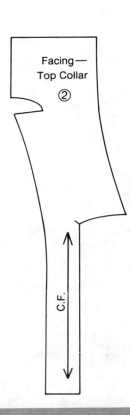

Facing —
Top Collar
②

C.F.

Stand Shawl Collar

Design Features

■ Stand shawl collar with a shaped band detail
■ Semi-fitted princess-seamed jacket with peplum
■ Elbow-length dolman sleeves

Basic Patterns

■ The Stand Shawl Collar, **pages 168** and **169**
■ The Dolman Sleeve & Hip-Length Pattern, Fitted Silhouette, **page 46**

Drafts

Step 1

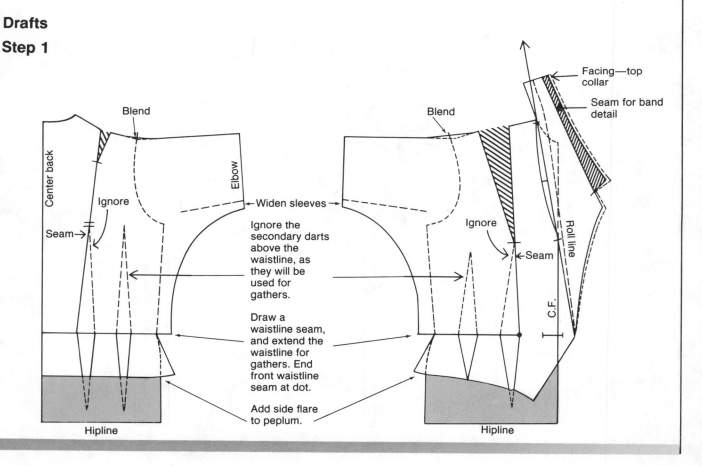

Blend

Center back

Elbow

Blend

Facing—top collar

Seam for band detail

Ignore

Roll line

Seam →

Widen sleeves

Ignore the secondary darts above the waistline, as they will be used for gathers.

Ignore

← Seam

Draw a waistline seam, and extend the waistline for gathers. End front waistline seam at dot.

C.F.

Add side flare to peplum.

Hipline

Hipline

Step 2 Peplums

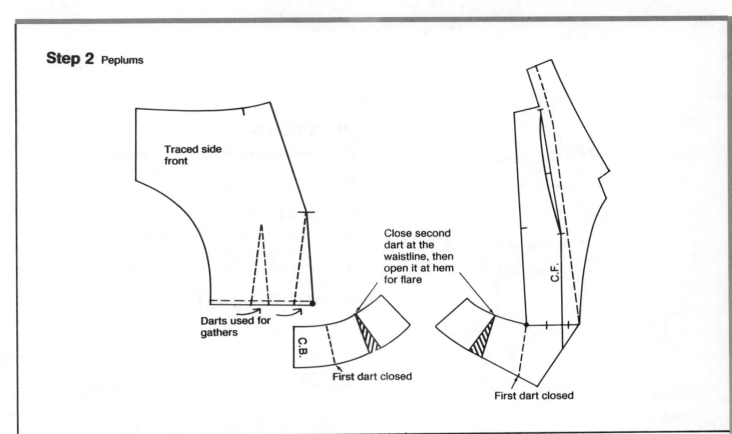

Traced side front

Darts used for gathers

Close second dart at the waistline, then open it at hem for flare

First dart closed

C.B.

C.F.

First dart closed

Patterns

(The final patterns have been reduced in scale.)

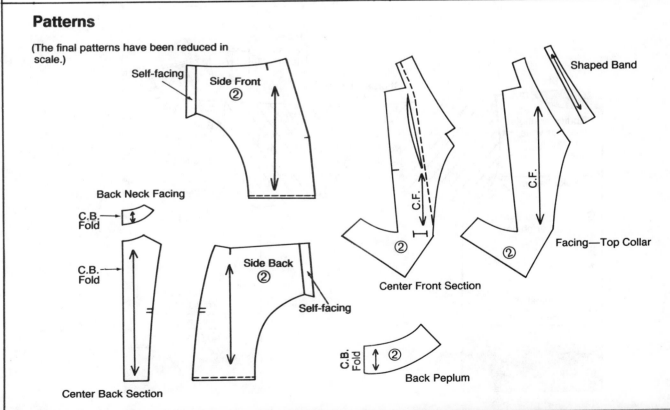

Self-facing

Side Front ②

Back Neck Facing

C.B. Fold

C.B. Fold

Center Back Section

Side Back ②

Self-facing

C.F. ②

Center Front Section

C.F. ②

Facing—Top Collar

Shaped Band

C.B. Fold ②

Back Peplum

Flat Shawl Collar with Standaway Neckline

Designed to Ease

Design Features

■ Flat standaway shawl collar on a yoke
■ Waist-length "big shirt" overblouse
■ Short sleeves

Basic Patterns

■ The Flat Shawl Collar with Standaway Neckline, **pages 184** and **185**
■ The "Big Shirt" Kimono Sleeve, **pages 108** and **109**
■ Armhole Seams, **page 12**

Drafts
Step 1

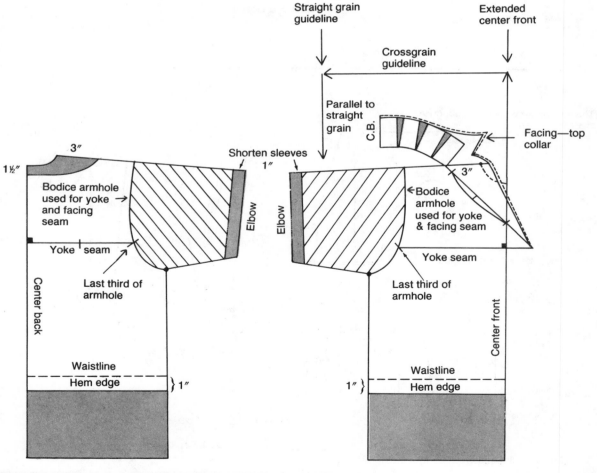

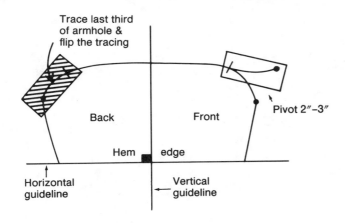

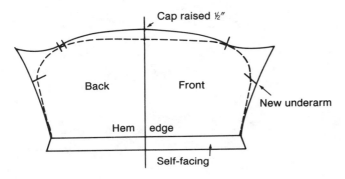

Step 2

A Trace and cut out the back and front sleeves (striped sections, Step 1).

B Draw a horizontal guideline and square a vertical guideline from it. Join the front and back sleeves so that their hems fall on the horizontal guideline and their overarms meet on the vertical guideline.

C Trace the last third of the front and back armholes and flip the tracings.

D Pivot the flipped-up tracing 2″–3″ between dots.

Step 3

A Draw new underarm seams to the hem edge. Add desired amount for self-facing.

B Raise the cap ½″ and blend to the crossmarks. (Double crossmarks for back.)

Patterns

The final patterns have been reduced in scale.

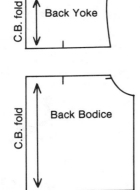

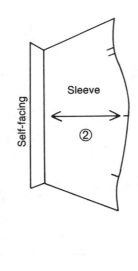

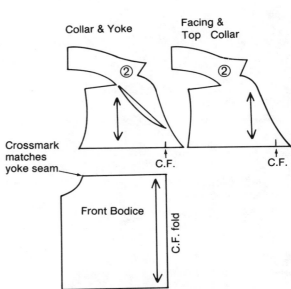

E*ight*

The Notch Collar

Stand Notch Collar with Basic Bodice Neckline

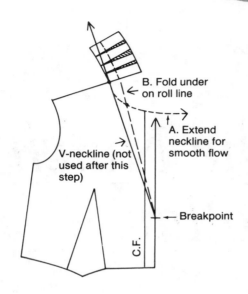

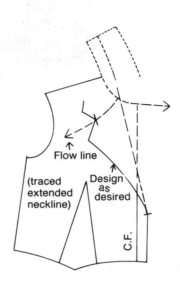

Step 1

The notch collar is basically the shawl collar with a neck seam, which serves to separate the collar and lapel sections. The separate collar can then be cut with its center back on fold; on various grains; and in fabrics different than the fabric used for the lapel and/or bodice. Also, the neck seam relieves the bubble-causing tension of the one-piece cut of the shawl collar, thus eliminating the need for the "fish" dart.

A Follow all of Steps 1 and 2, and Step 3, A and B, **pages 168** and **169.** Since the collar's seam will be an extension of the basic bodice neckline, it is important that that seam flows smoothly from the bodice for easy sewing of the collar to the bodice. Extend the basic bodice neckline several inches beyond center front, in a smooth, continuous curve.

B Once the roll line is drawn from the shoulder level to the breakpoint, fold the paper on that roll line so that the extended neckline is on top. Trace the extended neckline, and unfold the paper.

Step 2

The traced extended neckline will serve as a guide for the seam between the collar and the lapel, since it lies on the garment exactly where that seam will lie.

A Draw in the traced extended neckline. This line will now be referred to as the *flow line*.

B The seam on the garment will be visible from the roll line to the notch, and it can be any length desired. Determine the length desired, placing a mark on the flow line where the notch will begin.

C Design the lapel as desired from that mark to the breakpoint.

D Design the end of the collar as desired at the mark, which creates the notch at the same time.

Remember: When designing the length of the seam, and the shape of the lapel, collar and notch, the back of the collar has already been designed, and a proportion must be maintained between the front and back of the collar.

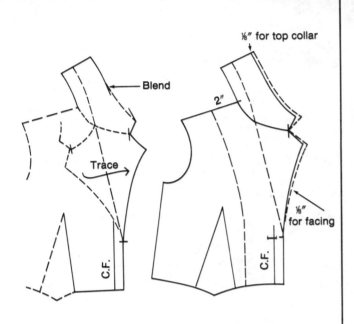

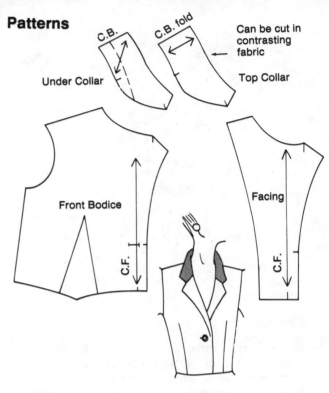

Patterns

Step 3

A Fold the paper under on the roll line so that the bodice is on top, and trace the designed lapel and the end of the collar, as well as the mark at the start of the notch. Unfold the paper. Blend a line for the outer edge of the collar connecting the back section to the front section of the collar. The front collar design may have to be adjusted slightly to accommodate a smoothly blended outer edge.

B For the bodice facing, which is also the top lapel, add ⅛″ (for medium-weight fabrics, less for lighter weights and more for heavier weights), starting at nothing at the notch and ending at nothing at the breakpoint. Mark off 2″ at the shoulder and draw a gently curved line from that mark to the waistline, ending near the dart, for the inner facing edge.

For the top collar, add ⅛″ at center back to nothing at the notch. Mark the buttonholes as desired, placing the first one at breakpoint level.

Patterns

A Trace the top collar. Label it to be cut on straight grain and on the fold at center back.

B Trace the under collar. The roll line is part of the under collar, as a guide for tailoring. Label the under collar to be cut on the bias, for a smoother fit, and with a center back seam, since that seam will be hidden.

C Trace the bodice and its facing as illustrated.

Roll Notch Collar with Basic Bodice Neckline

Step 1

The roll notch collar begins as the roll shawl collar, Steps 1 and 2, **page 170**. Continue with Step 3, A–E, **page 171**. When the back section of the roll shawl collar is completed, extend the basic bodice neckline several inches beyond center front, in a smooth continuous curve.

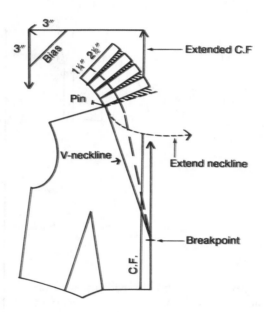

Step 2

Follow Step 1, B and C, **page 184**. Continued with Step 2, **page 184**.

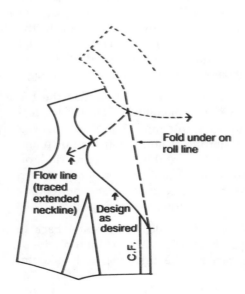

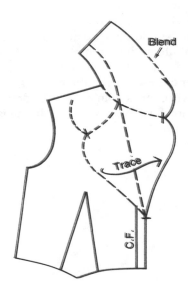

Follow Step 3, A, **page 189.**

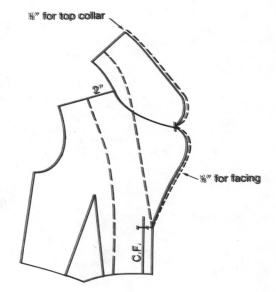

Follow Step 3, B, **page 189.**

Patterns

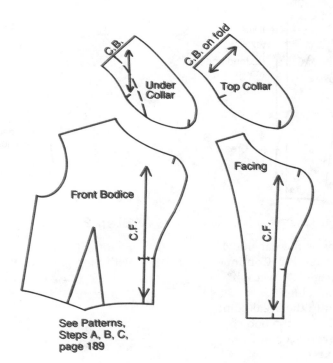

Flat Notch Collar with Basic Bodice Neckline

The flat notch collar will not have a stand at center back. However, all flat notch (and flat shawl) collars do develop at least a ½″ stand at the shoulder, due to the turning of the collar at that point. While this ½″ shoulder stand is not used during the drafting of the flat shawl collar, it is important in drafting the flat notch collar, since the roll line is vital to its construction.

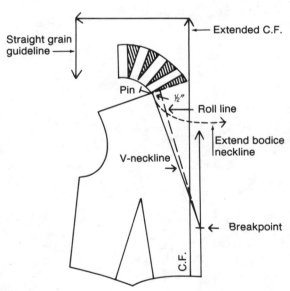

Step 1

The flat notch collar begins as the flat shawl collar, Step 1 and Step 2, **page 172.** Continue with Step 3, A, B and C, **page 173.** Mark ½″ stand out from the neck/shoulder intersection, and connect it to the breakpoint to establish the roll line. Extend the bodice neckline several inches beyond center front, in a smooth, continuous curve.

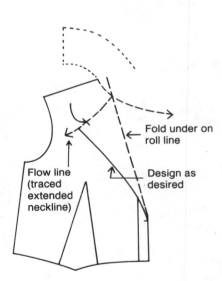

Step 2

Follow Step 1, B and C, **page 192.** Continue with Step 2, **page 192.**

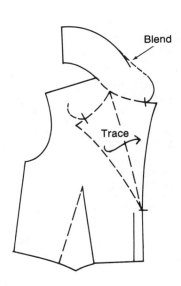

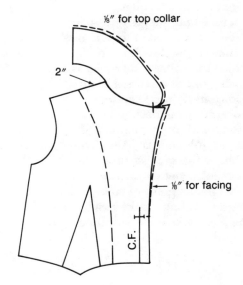

Step 3

Follow Step 3, A, **page 193.** Continue with
Step 3, B, **page 193.**

Patterns

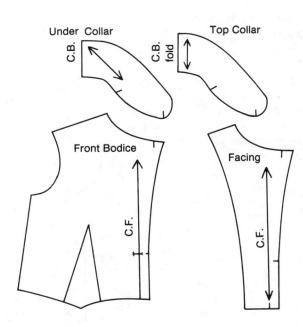

See Patterns, A,
B, and C, page
189.

Notch Collar with Lowered Neckline/Theory

All of the notch collars discussed on the previous pages have one important feature in common: the flow line on which the collar is designed is a tracing of the extended basic bodice neckline. Therefore, since the same neckline was used for all the variations (stand, roll and flat), they will all have the same seam on the garment, whether measured by its angle, its point of emergence on the roll line, or the height of the seam above the waistline.

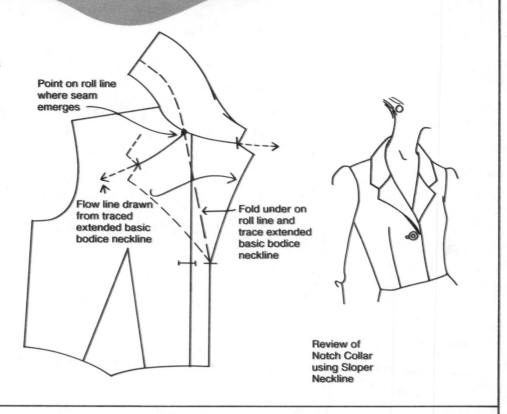

Point on roll line where seam emerges

Flow line drawn from traced extended basic bodice neckline

Fold under on roll line and trace extended basic bodice neckline

Review of Notch Collar using Sloper Neckline

In order to vary this common feature, the neckline must be lowered, since the neckline is the basis for the seam. It is best to first choose the point on the roll line where the seam emerges. The neckline is then drawn as a smooth curve from the shoulder to that point, and then extended indefinitely beyond it. Lowering the neckline this way changes the angle of the seam, the point on the roll line where it emerges, and the height of the seam above the waistline *as desired*.

The step-by-step method of developing the lowered neckline follows, **page 195**.

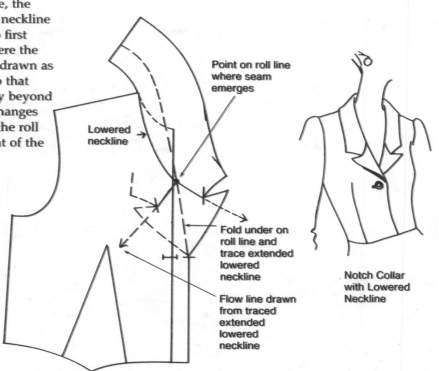

Point on roll line where seam emerges

Lowered neckline

Fold under on roll line and trace extended lowered neckline

Flow line drawn from traced extended lowered neckline

Notch Collar with Lowered Neckline

Notch Collar with Lowered Neckline/Method

Well, Flow Me Down!

The lowered neckline can be designed on any notch collar.

For the stand notch collar, follow all the steps on **pages 188** and **189,** designing and tracing the lowered neckline as part of Step 1.

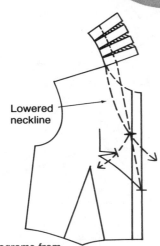

Lowered neckline

Diagrams from Steps 1 and 2, page 188

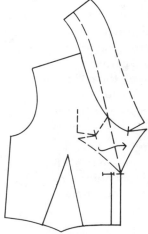

Step 3, A, page 189

Stand Collar

For the roll notch collar, follow all the steps on **pages 190** and **191,** designing and tracing the lowered neckline when referring to Step 1, **page 188.**

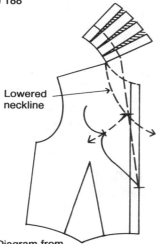

Lowered neckline

Diagram from Step 1 and 2, page 188

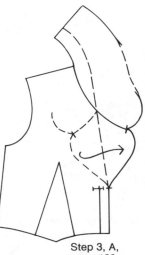

Step 3, A, page 189

Roll Collar

For the flat notch collar, follow all the steps on **pages 192** and **193,** designing and tracing the lowered neckline when referring to Step 1, **page 188.**

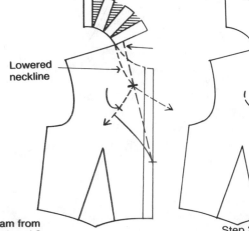

Lowered neckline

Diagram from Steps 1 and 2, page 190

Step 3, A, page 191

Flat Collar

Split Notch Collar

The split notch collar is one in which the notch design begins on the roll line itself. Since there is no seam on the garment connecting the collar and lapel, the collar can be turned up at the back neck without pulling the lapel with it. Also, the lapel can be closed without pulling the collar.

For split notch collar designs, the steps concerned with tracing the extended neckline and drawing the flow line (broken lines in illustrations) are unnecessary, since there is no seam beyond the roll line.

Follow the steps for the stand, roll or flat notch collar desired, omitting any reference to extending and tracing the neckline.

Design the collar and lapel from the same point selected on the roll line for the lowered neckline, or from the point where the bodice neckline crosses the roll line, if the neckline is not lowered. (The roll line crossmark replaces the notch crossmark.) Fold on the roll line and trace the collar and lapel.

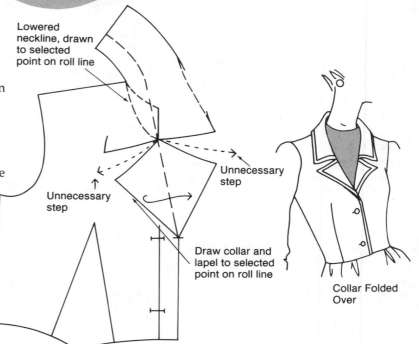

Lowered neckline, drawn to selected point on roll line

Unnecessary step

Unnecessary step

Draw collar and lapel to selected point on roll line

Collar Folded Over

Split Notch Collar shown as a Roll Collar

Patterns
(Facing not Included)

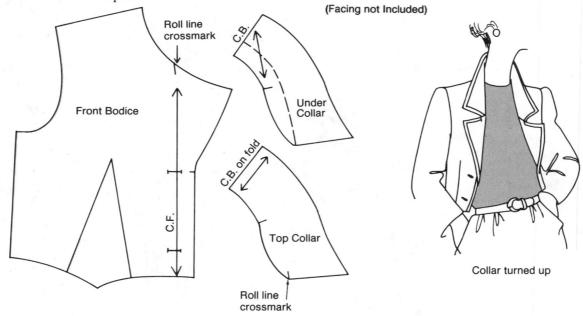

Roll line crossmark

Front Bodice

C.F.

C.B.

Under Collar

C.B. on fold

Top Collar

Roll line crossmark

Collar turned up

Notch Collar with Standaway Neckline

Draft

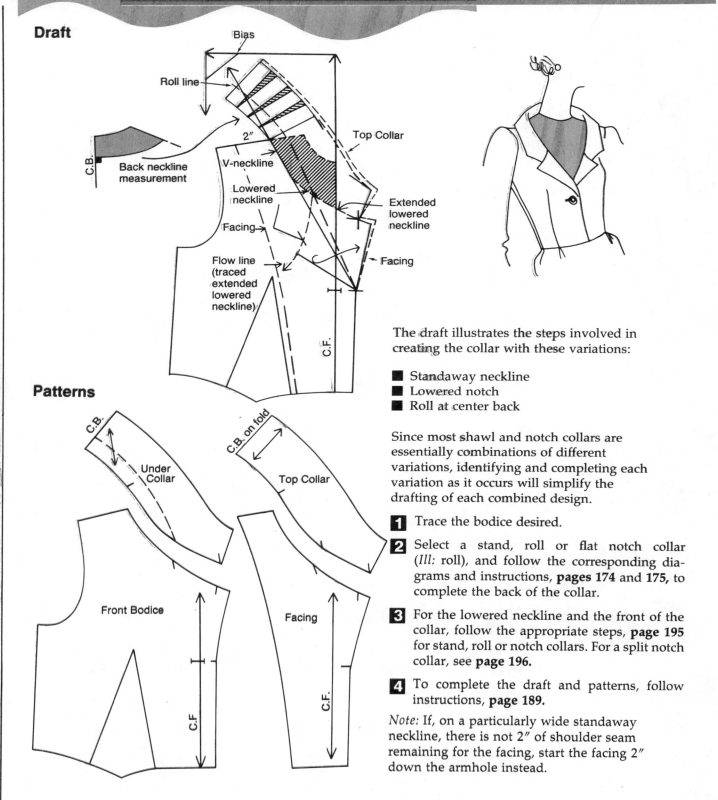

Patterns

The draft illustrates the steps involved in creating the collar with these variations:

- Standaway neckline
- Lowered notch
- Roll at center back

Since most shawl and notch collars are essentially combinations of different variations, identifying and completing each variation as it occurs will simplify the drafting of each combined design.

1 Trace the bodice desired.

2 Select a stand, roll or flat notch collar (*Ill:* roll), and follow the corresponding diagrams and instructions, **pages 174** and **175**, to complete the back of the collar.

3 For the lowered neckline and the front of the collar, follow the appropriate steps, **page 195** for stand, roll or notch collars. For a split notch collar, see **page 196**.

4 To complete the draft and patterns, follow instructions, **page 189**.

Note: If, on a particularly wide standaway neckline, there is not 2" of shoulder seam remaining for the facing, start the facing 2" down the armhole instead.

Design Variations

Stand Notch Collar

DESIGN VARIATION

Design Features

■ Stand notch collar with peaked lapels
■ Double-breasted semi-fitted dress
■ Short kimono sleeves

Basic Patterns

■ The Stand Notch Collar, **pages 188 and 189**
■ The Kimono Sleeve & Hip-Length Pattern,
  Semi-Fitted Silhouette, **page 21**

Drafts

Step 1

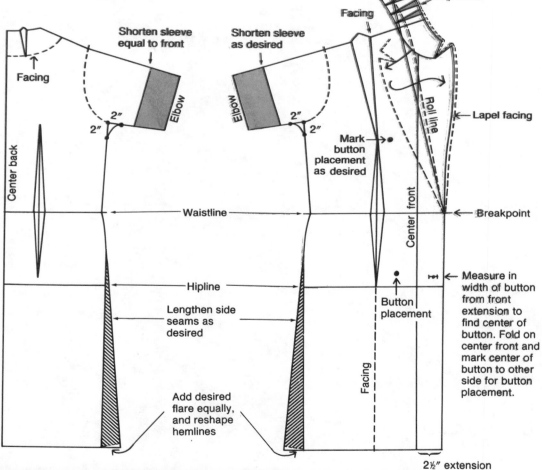

Shorten sleeve equal to front

Facing

Shorten sleeve as desired

Facing

Top collar

Roll line

Lapel facing

Elbow

Elbow

2"

2"

2"

2"

Center back

Mark button placement as desired

Center front

Breakpoint

Waistline

Hipline

Lengthen side seams as desired

Button placement

Facing

Add desired flare equally, and reshape hemlines

Measure in width of button from front extension to find center of button. Fold on center front and mark center of button to other side for button placement.

2½" extension

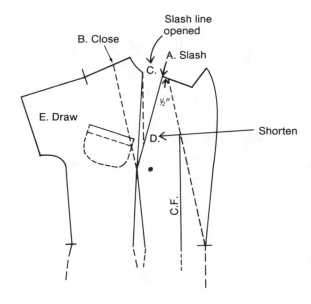

Slash line opened

B. Close

A. Slash

C.

E. Draw

½"

D.

Shorten

C.F.

Step 2

A Slash a line from the neck to the apex, starting ½" away from the roll line.

B Close the shoulder dart.

C Slash line opens to become a neck dart.

D Shorten the neck dart an amount that will conceal it under the collar and lapel.

E Draw welt pocket placement.

Patterns

The final patterns have been reduced in scale.

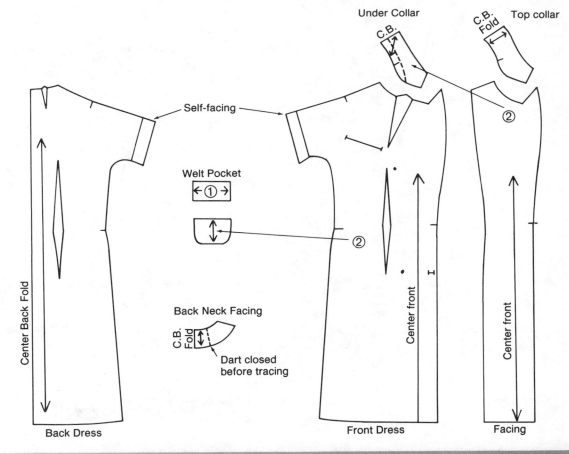

Self-facing

Under Collar

C.B.

C.B. Fold   Top collar

②

Welt Pocket

← ① →

②

Center Back Fold

Back Neck Facing

C.B. Fold

Dart closed before tracing

Center front

Center front

Back Dress

Front Dress

Facing

Low Notch Collar with Standaway Neckline

DESIGN VARIATION

- Low notch collar with standaway neckline on a waist-length dress jacket
- Double-breasted closing
- Three-quarter length batwing sleeves with separate cuffs

Basic Patterns

- The Roll Notch Collar with Standaway Neckline, **page 197**
- The Batwing Sleeve & Fitted Bodice, **page 66**

**Drafts
Step 1**

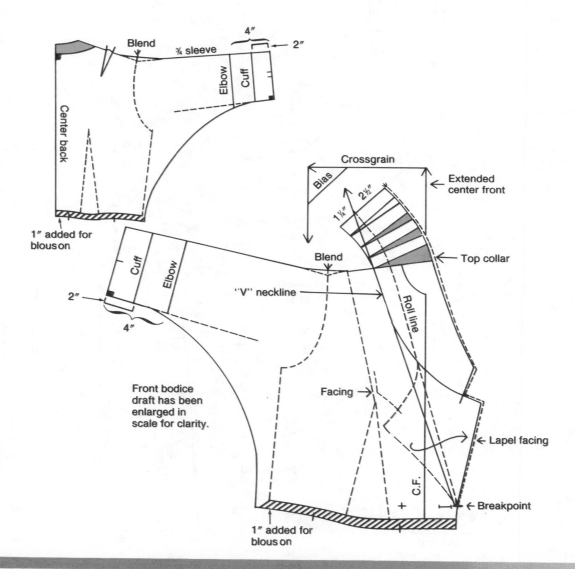

Blend
¾ sleeve
4″
2″
Elbow
Cuff
Center back
1″ added for blouson

Crossgrain
Bias
2½″
1¼″
Extended center front
Top collar
Cuff
Elbow
2″
4″
Blend
"V" neckline
Roll line
Front bodice draft has been enlarged in scale for clarity.
Facing
Lapel facing
C.F.
Breakpoint
1″ added for blouson

Step 2. Cuff

A Trace the back and front cuffs, and cut them out.

B Place the cuff's top edges on a fold of paper, joining them at the overarm seams. Trace the pattern.

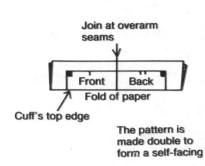

Join at overarm seams

Front | Back

Fold of paper

Cuff's top edge

The pattern is made double to form a self-facing

Patterns

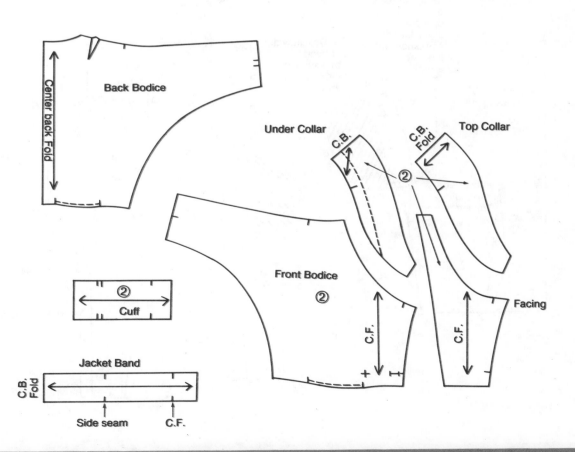

Back Bodice

Center back Fold

Under Collar

C.B.

C.B. Fold

Top Collar

②

Front Bodice

②

C.F.

C.F.

Facing

②

Cuff

Jacket Band

C.B. Fold

Side seam

C.F.

DESIGN VARIATION

Design Features

■ Flat notch collar joining the lapels without the conventional notch. The lapels have decorative top stitching.
■ Short kimono sleeves with shaped bands

Basic Patterns

■ The Flat Notch Collar, **pages 192** and **193**
■ The Kimono Sleeve, **page 7**

Drafts

Step 1

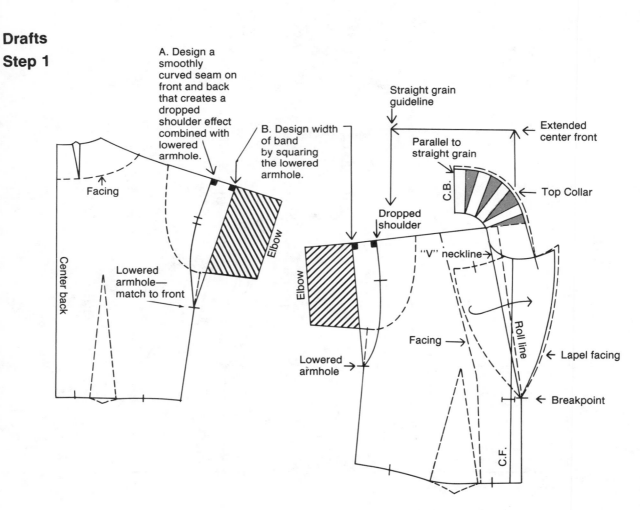

A. Design a smoothly curved seam on front and back that creates a dropped shoulder effect combined with lowered armhole.

B. Design width of band by squaring the lowered armhole.

Facing

Center back

Lowered armhole— match to front

Elbow

Straight grain guideline

Extended center front

Parallel to straight grain

C.B.

Top Collar

Dropped shoulder

Elbow

"V" neckline

Lowered armhole

Facing

Roll line

Lapel facing

Breakpoint

C.F.

Step 2 Shaped Sleeve Band

Trace back and front sleeve bands and cut them out. Place band edges on fold of paper, joining them at overarm seams. Trace pattern.

The pattern is made double to form a self-facing.

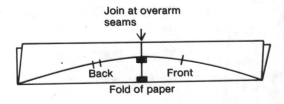

Join at overarm seams

Back   Front

Fold of paper

Patterns

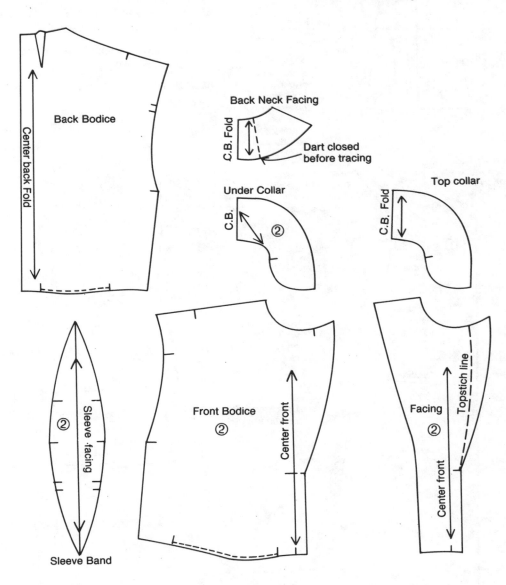

Back Bodice

Center back Fold

Back Neck Facing

C.B. Fold

Dart closed before tracing

Under Collar

C.B.

②

Top collar

C.B. Fold

Sleeve facing

②

Sleeve Band

Front Bodice
②

Center front

Facing
②

Center front

Topstich line

Split Notch Collar with Standaway Neckline

DESIGN VARIATION

Design Features

■ Lowered roll notch collar on a standaway neckline
■ Split lapels that can be button closed
■ Flared kimono dress with short sleeves

Basic Patterns

■ The Split Notch Collar, **page 196**
■ The Notch Collar with Standaway Neckline, **page 197**
■ The Kimono Sleeve & Hip-Length Pattern, Flared Silhouette, **page 21**

Note: Pivot back shoulder dart into flare at hem.

■ The Kimono Sleeve with Armhole Seam, **page 12**

Drafts Step 1

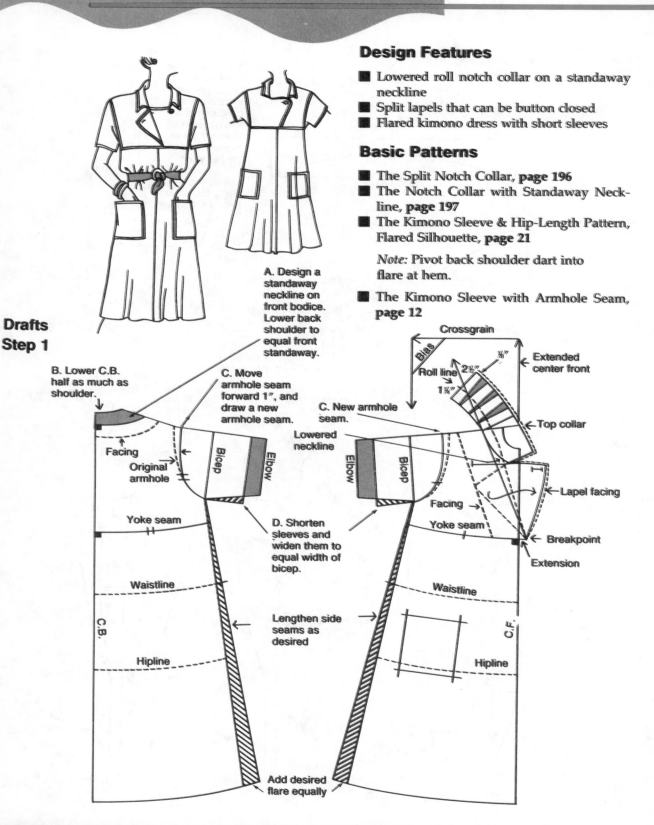

A. Design a standaway neckline on front bodice. Lower back shoulder to equal front standaway.

B. Lower C.B. half as much as shoulder.

C. Move armhole seam forward 1″, and draw a new armhole seam.

Facing

Original armhole

Bicep

Elbow

Yoke seam

Waistline

C.B.

Hipline

Add desired flare equally

C. New armhole seam.

Lowered neckline

Elbow

Bicep

D. Shorten sleeves and widen them to equal width of bicep.

Lengthen side seams as desired

Waistline

Hipline

C.F.

Crossgrain

Bias

Roll line

2½″

⅛″

1¼″

Extended center front

Top collar

Lapel facing

Facing

Yoke seam

Breakpoint

Extension

Step 2

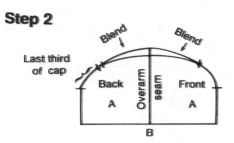

Trace the front and back sleeve sections.

A Place the front and back sections of the sleeve together along the overarm seam.

B Raise the cap ½″ and blend a line to the last third of the cap, front and back.c

Step 3

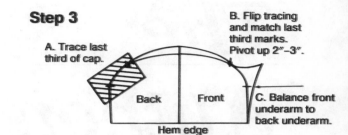

A Trace the last third of the cap, front and back, onto separate pieces of paper (illustrated here only on back).

B Flip each paper over, touching the "last third" marks to each other, and pivot the tracing up 2″–3″. Draw smoothly curved new underarm seams to the hem edge (illustrated here only on front).

C Balance the underarm seams.

Patterns

The final patterns have been reduced in scale.

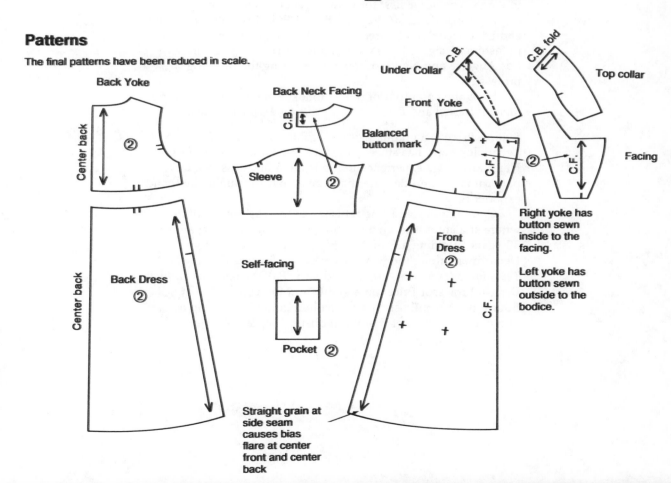

D E S I G N   V A R I A T I O N

About The Authors

Bernard Zamkoff is a Professor of Fashion Design at the Fashion Institute of Technology in New York City, where he has concentrated on the teaching of flat pattern design since 1964.

He served as the Chairman of the Fashion Design Department of FIT from 1978 through 1984, and has been recognized for his contributions to education by his being listed in *Who's Who in the East* for several years in succession.

Professor Zamkoff is a graduate of Pratt Institute, where he earned a Bachelor's Degree in Fine Arts, with Honors, majoring in fashion design. He was a designer for several years in both Los Angeles and New York, before entering the teaching profession.

He is the co-author of the textbooks *Grading Techniques for Modern Design* and *Basic Pattern Skills for Fashion Design*.

Jeanne Price is a graduate of the Fashion Institute of Technology and has since gained a Bachelor of Science Degree. Her many years experience in the fashion business as a buyer, patternmaker, and designer have given her invaluable firsthand experience.

Coming full circle, she returned to the Fashion Institute where she embarked on a teaching career which has spanned 30 years, attaining a Professorship in the Fashion Design Department along the way. Besides co-authoring *Grading Techniques for Modern Design* and *Basic Pattern Skills for Fashion Design*, Professor Price, on a grant from the U.S. Office of Education, has published a curriculum guide to Grading as part of a five-part series of Fashion Industry Program Guides.